SOUTHERN WRITERS

SOUTHERN WRITERS

Photographs by
DAVID G. SPIELMAN

Text by
WILLIAM W. STARR

Foreword by
FRED HOBSON

 UNIVERSITY OF SOUTH CAROLINA PRESS

Photographs © 1997 David G. Spielman
Text © 1997 William W. Starr
Foreword © 1997 Fred Hobson

Published in Columbia, South Carolina, by the
University of South Carolina Press

Printed in Hong Kong

01 00 99 98 97   5 4 3 2

Permission to reproduce any image included in this book must be obtained in writing from:
David G. Spielman, Post Office Box 15741, New Orleans, LA 70175.

Library of Congress Cataloging-in-Publication Data

Spielman, David G., 1950–
      Southern writers / photographs by David G. Spielman; text by William W. Starr;
    foreword by Fred Hobson.
          p.   cm.
      ISBN 1–57003–224–6
      1. Authors, American—Southern States—Portraits. 2. Authors, American—Southern States—
    Interviews. 3. Authors, American—20th century—Interviews. 4. Authors, American—20th century
    Portraits. 5. Southern States—Intellectual life—1865– 6. Southern States—In literature. 7. Authorship.
    I. Starr, William W., 1940– . II. Title.
    PS261.S64 1997
    810.9'975—dc21
      [B]   97–4914

For Catherine Mayer-Spielman,
painter, wife, friend for life.

In memory of J. Stone Coulter
and Robert Morton, creative mentors.
D. G. S.

For Carol, first and specially.
And for Amy and Francis, Heidi, Erik and Karl.
W. W. S.

FOREWORD

Fred Hobson

What we usually get with writers, Southern or otherwise, is the product of their work—the books—but, unlike actors, ballerinas, tight-rope walkers, and basketball players, we see little of the process, the action of the work in progress. We are given the books and, on occasion, we are given the persona, the writer, as he or she appears at readings, signings, award ceremonies, and so forth.

What we have here, in *Southern Writers*, is much more. There's still the somewhat contrived persona, of course—the writer choosing where and how, in what and with what to be photographed—but nearly all of David G. Spielman's engaging shots are taken on the writer's native ground. William W. Starr's biographical sketches accompanying the photographs *are* about the process—not just what but when and where and how, and sometimes even why, a particular writer writes. A primary revelation in all this is that writing isn't as easy as it sometimes seems—that behind a free-flowing and captivating narrative often lies agony. "I have to practically have a gun to my head to force me to write," says Lee Smith, who at age fifty-two has produced some twelve novels and whose relaxed, folksy demeanor at readings and other public appearances gives anything but that impression. "I hate it. It's work, so much work." It's work, and it's a solitary activity. Writers always have to be on call, awaiting the muse. Some rise early and hang on grimly, Josephine Humphreys at 4:30 A.M., Fred Chappell at 5:30, many others also well before sunrise. But Julie Smith can write only *after* 4 P.M. And so on.

It's so much work—and conditions have to be just right—that writers, as they reveal here, do a number of things to help the process along. Novelist Clyde Edgerton rents a small, windowless basement room that will offer absolutely no distractions. Novelist Terry Kay holes up in cheap motels. A couple of other writers, living on the Atlantic coast with beautiful bay views, turn their desks away from the windows, from temptation. Others take their phones off the hook or, while writing, take messages only on answering machines. At least one novelist I know has a white-noise maker, euphemistically called a "sound conditioner," with which he drowns out all sounds, good and bad, except the various voices of his own making. Writers may hate to write—in truth, all of them don't, and certainly not all the time—yet they *have* to write, are compelled not only to "tell about the South" (as a Faulkner character puts it in *Absalom, Absalom!)* but also to tell about people and places and events that may or may not be Southern but whose significance, in any case, goes far beyond the South. As Eudora Welty, now eighty-eight and plagued by arthritis, says here, "If worse comes to worse, I'd write with my teeth."

The subjects here write in nearly every way short of that—sitting, standing, lying down. Most now compose on computers, but hardly all. As one who (Bill Clinton's bridge to the twenty-first century notwithstanding) has barely been led, technologically speaking, kicking and screaming into the late twentieth, I am encouraged to learn that a large number of these writers still compose at the typewriter, or even in longhand. Age seems to make little difference in this respect. Richard Ford, Sheila Bosworth, Pat Conroy, and John Dufresne, all comparatively young, write their books, at least their first drafts, with pen or pencil, as do the more seasoned William Styron, Shelby Foote, George Garrett, Willie Morris, and many others. But John Hope Franklin, at age eighty-one, works on a computer.

It's details such as these that I find fascinating in William Starr's sketches, and we are told as well what—besides writers—many of these writers are or have been: firefighters (Larry Brown), carpenters (Lawrence Naumoff), physicians (Ferrol Sams and John Stone), peach farmers (Dori Sanders), shrimpers (William Baldwin), preachers (Will Campbell), fighter pilots (Clyde Edgerton), karate black belts (Christine Wiltz), snake handlers (Tim McLaurin), and, as you might expect, a few newspaper reporters and university professors. These writers range in age from their mid-thirties to late eighties (Welty), they are principally (but not altogether) fiction writers, and they hail from all parts of Dixie, from the Potomac to the Sabine, from the Ohio to the Gulf, with the Carolinas and Louisiana seeming to seize a slight numerical advantage.

And what of the photographs themselves? We can tell a great deal about the writers by how they face the camera: Elizabeth Spencer, Will Campbell, and Barry Hannah (the sanguine Mississippians) all smiling broadly, Fred Chappell looking somewhat mischievous, Doris Betts and Roy Blount, Jr., rather pensive—and Clyde Edgerton barefoot. Many of the subjects are in their studies or libraries, standing in front of a shelf of books, or sitting at (or, in Patricia Cornwell's case, *on*) desks. Anne Rice, in her cluttered study, is surrounded by books, papers, a stuffed owl, a miniature Elvis, and Mardi Gras beads. James Lee Burke holds his guitar. Others stand in their yards and gardens, and some are on front porches—which seems altogether appropriate since so much Southern storytelling has originated there. Most of all, the way these writers are dressed is telling—as compared, say, to a book of this sort done thirty years ago. Of the four dozen or so males included, only two are wearing ties, and many women are dressed similarly in informal fashion. Richard Ford, Bobbie Ann Mason, and many others wear jeans.

9

What strikes me most of all—again compared to, say, a half-century ago—is how many of these Southern writers actually live and work in the *South*. If a David Spielman predecessor had put together a similar volume in the 1940s, he would have had to spend a lot of time in New York City and environs photographing his subjects. That's where the publishing houses were, and that's where the finest universities were. Many still are, but not all, and thus the Southern writer can live on the Carolina coast or in the Piedmont, in the Mississippi Delta or piney hills, in the Ozarks or on the Louisiana bayou without being cut off altogether from the world of letters. Of the seventy or so writers gathered here (three or four of whom were born outside the South) only two, Roy Blount, Jr., and James Wilcox, live principally in New York City, and only a handful of others live outside the South at all. Thomas Wolfe could now come home again, Willie Morris *did* come home again, and so did the distinguished African American historian John Hope Franklin and the award-winning African American novelist Margaret Walker. "I live in an historic area here," Walker says of her neighborhood in Jackson, Mississippi. "This house is right between Martin Luther King Boulevard and Medgar Evers Street. Doesn't get any better."

PHOTOGRAPHER'S NOTE

My goal in this book has been to offer something other than dust-cover photos. I wanted to show writers "at home"—in their houses or neighborhoods, at signings or book festivals, and, most of all, in their own work spaces pictured exactly as the authors themselves find them each time they come to take up the writing process. Many authors had told me stories of how photographers had claimed hours of their time, interrupted their lives, and disrupted their work. It was my aim to travel light and work quickly, to spend brief but significant periods of time with these authors to capture them as they spent their days or nights writing or on tour and to produce in the process a collection of informal and revealing portraits.

To achieve a natural effect, for lighting I used a combination of what was available on site, along with some portable, battery-operated strobes. My cameras are Leica rangefinders; the lenses used were 35mm, 50mm, and 90mm, the film Tri-X and Neopan 1600.

With a few exceptions, these portraits were shot within a period of 210 days. I drove over 40,000 miles and flew I'm not sure how many. My hope is that these photos show natural expression—the writers, their spaces, and *not* the photographer's idea of these. If I have erred, may it be on the side of spontaneity, not overproduction.

D. G. S.

ACKNOWLEDGMENTS

It is a privilege to thank first and foremost the authors who gave so freely of their time and were so very supportive and willing.

Thanks also to the independent booksellers who helped me track down some of the authors and provided background information that was beneficial in understanding the subjects: Richard and Lisa Howorth of Square Books, Oxford, Mississippi; Britton Trice of Garden District Books, New Orleans, Louisiana; and John Evans of Lemuria Bookstore, Jackson, Mississippi.

And, finally, special thanks are due Catherine Fry whose many years of support made this project possible. Her knowledge and perception have greatly enriched this work.

D. G. S.

SOUTHERN WRITERS

TINA MCELROY ANSA tells the story of a fan who came to her at a recent book signing and said in a gush of praise, "I loved your new book. I read it in just a few hours last night." Ansa rolled her eyes, grabbed the woman, and told her, "Dammit, it took me six years to write that book. Can't you take a few more hours to get through it?" She tells the story with a smile, acknowledging how wonderful it is to have readers who care so much. Ansa, who grew up in Macon, Georgia, and worked for newspapers in Atlanta and Charlotte, is intense, serious, wildly funny, and charming—and one of the most acclaimed young writers in America. She was photographed on a mild November morning at her cottage on Plum Broke Road on St. Simons Island, Georgia. She lives there with her husband Jonee, a filmmaker, and together they have served as directors of the Georgia Sea Island Festival. Their unusually comfortable home is decorated with an abundance of primitive art, much of it made on the island, and is filled with green plants, wild flowers, icons from friends and family—and cats. Outside is a small house where her husband does his work, and a hot tub, where both can relax and unwind at the end of a busy day. Ansa's first novel, *Baby of the Family*, a young woman's coming-of-age story set in a small Georgia town in the 1950s, was published in 1989 and was named a Notable Book of the Year by the *New York Times*. It was followed by *Ugly Ways* (1993) and *The Hand I Fan With* (1996), both novels narrated with the vivid humor which also is a staple of the author's popular public appearances. Her work, rich in African American folklore and rhythms, has been widely anthologized.

WILLIAM "BILLY" BALDWIN has spent almost all of his fifty years in the same place: the tiny coastal village of McClellanville between Charleston and Myrtle Beach, South Carolina. There he's been a shrimper, an oysterman, a teacher, a local historian, a builder of both boats and houses, and, most recently, a writer. His first novel, *The Hard to Catch Mercy*, was published in 1993. Its completion was interrupted by Hurricane Hugo, which roared through South Carolina and dealt McClellanville a near-fatal blow in the fall of 1989. The shy, soft-spoken Baldwin spent most of the next three years helping his neighbors rebuild their shattered homes. His own, constructed in 1982, was damaged but survived Hugo's waters and wind, though his dock did not. "I just didn't ever get around to repairing my own place," he says. When *The Hard to Catch Mercy* did arrive—a funny, epic tale set in 1916 in a Lowcountry fishing village not unlike McClellanville—it won the 1993 Lillian Smith Award for fiction. In accepting the award, he declared, "I believe in the perhaps now unfashionable notion of the indomitable and enduring. I believe that all life is sacred . . . and that skin color, sex, and sexual preference are simply veneers overlaying an equally old-fashioned concept of all-encompassing life force." The author looks back on a "dysfunctional" past and ahead to a future "with more writing. I can't imagine doing anything else." He pauses for the photographer on the refurbished dock behind the house he lives in with his wife Lil. "It's pretty rickety; shows you what kind of a builder I am." His second novel, *The Fennel Family Papers,* a satire also set in the Lowcountry, came out in 1996.

MADISON SMARTT BELL was a difficult author to photograph, though not for any lack of helpfulness on his part. There were plans to see him during the 1996 Southern Festival of Books in Nashville, not far from his hometown of Franklin. But Bell's mother was ill on the farm, and his schedule was quickly changed. Then there was a tightly packed book tour for his just-published novel *Ten Indians*, which took him from Washington, D.C., to Los Angeles and Portland. But he found a few minutes in the middle of the hectic tour schedule in Oxford, Mississippi, shortly before a book signing and reading attended by local writers Larry Brown and Barry Hannah. "Yeah, it's good to see them there," he said. "That kind of support among writers isn't something you see all the time." He posed outside a small African American church near Oxford, perhaps an appropriate site in view of the fact that his acclaimed novel *All Souls' Rising* (1995) focuses on a rebellion by black slaves in Haiti. Since his first book, *The Washington Square Ensemble,* was released in 1983, Bell—only thirty-nine now—has published eight novels and a pair of short-story collections at an amazing rate of nearly one a year. He's won praise from reviewers around the United States and was recently named one of the "best young American novelists under forty" by Granta. He was Phi Beta Kappa at Princeton University, where he won several literary awards and studied with various writers, including George Garrett, whom he describes as having played an important role in his development. He lives in Baltimore with his wife, the poet Elizabeth Spires, and teaches at Goucher College. His first four novels are set in New York City or other urban areas, and it was not until *Soldier's Joy* in 1989 that he turned to the South as his fictional landscape. "I waited until I was ready to write about the South without coming under the influence of Southern writers who had done it all before and better than I ever could."

WENDELL BERRY was in the midst of a hectic schedule when he met the photographer at a bookstore in Lexington, Kentucky. He had agreed to sign books with two other Bluegrass State authors—Guy Davenport and Ed McClanahan—and was rushing to get out of town and to make arrangements to have some business matters cleared up at his farm. He posed in front of the store, breaking away repeatedly to greet old friends who showed up before his signing got under way. Berry, now sixty-two, published his first book, the novel *Nathan Coulter,* in 1960 and has written thirty-six volumes of fiction and nonfiction since then. Thematically, his books stress the relationship between people and the land, expressing a philosophy which he has integrated successfully in his life and his work. He was born at Port Royal, Kentucky, and has lived in his native state most of his life. However, he was living in and teaching in New York City in 1965 when he decided to return to Kentucky, moving his family to a working farm on July 4th of the next year. He has been there for the last thirty-one years, honing his belief that there is a difference between knowing and living in a place and "cherishing and living responsibly in it." Perhaps his most familiar work remains *The Unsettling of America* (1977), in which he offers a critique of agricultural policies and their devastating effects on farmers. Berry speaks with some casualness about his writing habits: "The best way for me is to write half a day and work outdoors half a day," he has said. He would prefer to write in the morning and go out in the afternoon during the winter months and reverse the schedule in the summer. He writes out his manuscripts with a pencil because "I erase a lot and cross out a lot."

DORIS BETTS doesn't write in her tiny, cramped office on the campus of the University of North Carolina at Chapel Hill. She does so some twenty-five miles away, with a typewriter, at her home, where she also spends time with her horses. "That's how I separate the parts of my life," she says. The habit "also comes from the time when I was a mother with kids at home." That's how she wrote her first book, a collection of stories, *The Gentle Insurrection* (1954). The office is where this Alumni Distinguished Professor of English devotes many hours weekly to teaching and counseling some of the hundreds of students who look to her for literary guidance. "I love working with beginning writers; they're not cocky yet, they're not jaded." With photographs of Elvis showering, a picture of a much-younger Betts, and a metal sign reading "Reserved Parking for Doris Betts," the office reflects the eclectic, spontaneous, and sometimes outrageous sense of humor of its occupant. Betts enjoys laughing. Now sixty-four, she enjoys respect and affection from her students, doesn't keep the first drafts of her books, and throws away all preliminary manuscripts. She keeps a supply of fine-point pens on her desk because "they are great for marking between the lines of student's papers," but when she writes in longhand, it is with a large, stylish fountain pen. The author of eight novels and short-story collections, the Statesville, North Carolina, native is very much at ease with her writing and her personal life: "And I would hope so; at my age you figure the worst that's going to happen has happened."

ROY BLOUNT, JR., spoofs presidents, puts together crossword puzzles, was president of his high-school class, and can spit watermelon seeds. He is, in the estimation of everyone who reads him, one of the funniest men in America, a burden that regrettably "doesn't make the process of writing any easier." Blount was born in Indianapolis, Indiana, but grew up near Atlanta, was educated at Vanderbilt and Harvard, and wrote for the *Atlanta Journal* before heading north to take a job with *Sports Illustrated* magazine. During his eight years there, he produced his first book, *About Three Bricks Shy of a Load* (1974), examining the 1973 season of the Pittsburgh Steelers. His apartment on Manhattan's Upper West Side—he also has a small home in western Massachusetts—has plenty of views: "If you stand outside and crane your neck you can almost see Central Park." The apartment's comfortable but a bit in disarray, and on a living room table crowded with books and papers, he is unable to locate a book he wants to show the visiting photographer. In his writing space he is at work on an autobiographical memoir: "I've been snagged on it for the last four years." The shelves are lined with books, and one wall displays posters, a colorful chart of fish found along the North Carolina coast, and the fairly unattractive head of a warthog. ("I didn't kill it; I bought it to give to a friend, and it didn't work out, so I kept it.") Blount has no specific writing regimen, though he confesses, "I really like to write late at night. When I did my first book I slept from nine until five and stayed up and wrote all night. It was wonderful. I can't do that any more." Blount has written eleven books, uncounted poems and doggerel, comic songs, and even a pair of one-act plays. His output includes collections of humorous essays that deal with the South through the eyes of a Southerner (*Cracker*, published in 1980), and he is the editor of *Roy Blount's Book of Southern Humor* (1994). His first novel, *First Hubby*, the entertaining story of a man married to the nation's first female president, appeared in 1990.

SHEILA BOSWORTH was born in New Orleans and has lived in or close to the city for most of her forty-seven years. She met the photographer in the living room of her home in Covington, Louisiana—not too far from the late Walker Percy's home—where she has lived for eleven years. She knew Percy and calls him "very generous" with his help early in her writing life. "When he got the bound galleys of my first book, he called me on the phone, and I was scared he wouldn't like it. He was always so honest, he would have told me that. But when I got on the phone, he said he was wondering if my husband would mind if he gave me a big hug. Wow! Talk about a thrill." For that first novel, *Almost Innocent* (1984), Percy compared Bosworth to Henry James and called the book "A lovely achievement, a superior one." Her novel also featured a glowing encomium from the poet James Dickey. "I had a very fortunate start," she says. "When I first saw a copy of that book, I thought, 'Who wrote this?' I could scarcely remember I did. It was like the Catholic grace—unearned." Her second novel, *Slow Poison*, wasn't released until 1992, but that, she explains, was the fault of publisher's schedules and not her own writing habits. "That was the worst part of being a published writer. Everyone kept asking when my next book would be out. It got to be a little embarrassing." Bosworth has no defined writing area. "I started writing when I had two small children, so I wrote anywhere I could put a yellow legal pad, my pen, and a thesaurus. I'd write and the kids would just bounce off the walls." Her favorite part of the creative process, however, is revising, which she calls "fun." As a youngster, she was a voracious reader: "Books were my drug of choice." An English major in college, she always thought about writing, "though it never became a compulsion. I did it because that's what I did."

LARRY BROWN lives on a working farm at Yacona, Mississippi, not far from Oxford and close to the little community of Potlockney, where he was born in 1951. He burst onto the literary scene in 1988 with a stunning short-story collection, *Facing the Music*, written while he was a full-time firefighter in Oxford. He quit that job two years later "Because I wanted to be known as Larry Brown the writer, not Larry Brown the fireman." By then he had a novel, *Dirty Work,* published and was on his way to an important writing career. He remains largely unchanged by his growing success, though he finds it difficult to meet the mounting requests for his time. "All those people wanting a little bit. It's great, but I can't do that and write, too." At his public readings, he has brought audiences to tears with the unflinching vision of his prose. He was doing some work on his house when he paused to pose for the photographer on a warm late-September morning. He initially was reluctant to move into his writing space because "the whole house is a big mess," but he later showed the place in the small bedroom where he works. Described by one friend as a "heavy-smokin', guitar-playing, good ol' boy," Brown writes with a terse, honest, hard edge and a Southern writer's keen ear for the voices of the desperate. He has completed six books, including three novels (most recently *Father and Son* in 1996), two short-story collections, and one volume of essays about his life as a firefighter (*On Fire,* 1993). He has spent his life in Mississippi except for a ten-year period in his youth when he was in Memphis and a stint in the Marine Corps in the early 1970s. He had to repeat an English course in high school and decided when he was nearly thirty to become a writer. He virtually taught himself, enduring numerous rejections before successfully publishing short stories.

JAMES LEE BURKE found employment early in his life as an English instructor, a surveyor, a newspaper reporter, a worker with convicts in California and on an oil rig off the Louisiana coast. "I have a real embarrassing employment record," he says with a boyish smile. But always he knew he would be writing. And he always has. "I published my first story in 1956 when I was nineteen. I've spent all my life writing. That's been constant." But the path to publication has hardly been a smooth one. Burke's first novel, *Half of Paradise,* was released in 1965. Three more followed to no great success. Then Louisiana State University Press published two novels, *The Convict* (1985) and *The Lost Get-Back Boogie* (1986), and suddenly Burke was once again being courted by commercial publishers. "I really owe a lot to LSU Press. They came along when no one else was interested," he says. His popular Cajun Louisiana detective Dave Robicheaux made his first appearance in his next book, *Neon Rain,* in 1987 and has returned for encores in seven books, including *Heaven's Prisoners* (1988) and *In the Electric Mist with Confederate Dead* (1993). His latest Robicheaux novel is *Cadillac Jukebox* (1996). A native of Houston, Texas, Burke, sixty, now has homes in Missoula, Montana, and New Iberia, Louisiana. He met the photographer on a cold, snowy afternoon in the cozy, woodstove-heated home he's lived in near Missoula since 1989. There, with blues albums playing steadily on the stereo, he writes with great discipline, producing between one thousand and two thousand words on good days. "That's the only way I can pull it off." He also admits to keeping "funny hours" while he's writing, sometimes hitting the computer in the morning, sometimes in the evening. For relaxation, there's his guitar and some of the world's best fly-fishing only a few miles away—one of the reasons he's been coming to Montana for nearly thirty years.

ROBERT OLEN BUTLER AND ELIZABETH DEWBERRY

were married on Shakespeare's birthday, April 23, 1995, at the Tavern on the Green in Central Park in what was called "the literary wedding of the year." Butler, who won the Pulitzer Prize for Fiction for his 1992 story collection *A Good Scent from a Strange Mountain,* said the couple "fell in love reading each other's books. She read *They Whisper* and I read her *Break the Heart of Me.* Right away we knew we shared the same feelings, the same sensibilities. We met in July 1994 at the Sewanee Writer's Conference, and it took me all of twenty-four hours to propose." Butler and his wife, who was born in Birmingham, now live in Lake Charles, Louisiana, where Butler teaches at McNeese State University and "Betsy" writes full-time. They each have separate writing spaces in their home, so they agreed to pose for the photographer on a "neutral" site, sitting in an old American Renaissance bed that has what Butler calls "an astonishing headboard." Since 1981 Butler has published eight novels and *A Good Scent.* His latest book is another story collection, *Tabloid Dreams* (1996). His wife has completed two highly praised novels, *Many Things Have Happened Since He Died* in 1990 and *Break the Heart of Me* in 1994, both written when she used the last name of her first husband (she now scratches out his name when she signs copies of those books). She holds an English degree from Vanderbilt and a Ph.D. in American literature from Emory. For a brief period she taught at Ohio State but "loathed" the experience. "We're very comfortable and very happy in Lake Charles," Butler says. Each maintains at least one unusual hobby: he has a remarkable collection of antique fountain pens and is beginning to collect antique watches, while she collects antique jewelry made of pieces of human hair.

WILL CAMPBELL, seventy-two, wasn't feeling as good as he would like to have been when he met the photographer at his middle-Tennessee farm on a sunny October afternoon. His hand, just released from a heavy bandage, had been badly mangled in an accident he had while driving his tractor two weeks earlier. His sixty-acre rock-ribbed farm, not far from Nashville, has been home for Campbell and his wife Brenda since 1963. He and a friend built the log cabin, perhaps sixty yards from the main house, which, with its collection of hats and an old barber chair, serves as Campbell's office. "It's pretty much thrown together. He thought I knew what I was doing, and I thought he knew what he was doing." A tobacco chewer for most of his life—"My daddy got me started"—Campbell finally quit five months before posing for this photograph. Campbell grew up a poor farmer's son in the Mississippi Delta. Calling himself "a bootleg preacher," he was ordained a Southern Baptist minister when he was just seventeen. He went to Yale Divinity School and returned to his native South to become an outspoken activist in the civil rights movement and later a leader in efforts to aid impoverished whites in the region—some of them Ku Klux Klan members. Campbell's simple credo may be seen on a medal he wears around his neck, a globe with an equal sign. "It means we are all equal under the sun. . . . We are all sinners, and all equally deserving of help." At night "Brother Will" has been known to strum his guitar and softly sing songs about Southern guilt and misunderstanding. A poet, songwriter, and performer as well as an author, Campbell wrote a widely acclaimed, poignant, lyric self-analysis entitled *Brother to a Dragonfly* in 1977. His latest book, *The Stem of Jesse* (1995), is a true story of rejection and redemption at a Southern Baptist college.

FRED CHAPPELL, one of America's genuine men of letters, writes in two places in the Greensboro, North Carolina, home he and his wife Susan have lived in for more than three decades. He's usually up at 5:30 in the morning, when he heads downstairs to the kitchen, makes coffee, and begins working in longhand on top of a butcher block. When Susan wakes and comes down for her breakfast, he returns to their bedroom, where he has a small, uncommonly neatly arranged alcove, and continues writing in longhand. "I'll work anywhere from seven to nine o'clock, then head for school," he says. Chappell, sixty, can't resist making some disparaging remarks about his schedule, but that's a reflection of his keen sense of the comic, which informs many of his poems, stories, and novels. Born in Canton, North Carolina, in the mountainous western section of the state that he has used as a setting for much of his work, Chappell has remained within the state's borders throughout his career. His first published book, the novel *It Is Time, Lord,* appeared in 1963, the first of six novels followed by two books of short stories, thirteen volumes of poetry, an anthology, and a book of essays. His most ambitious project is a four-volume autobiography in verse, *Midquest,* written, he says, in the tradition of his model, Dante. The poetry achieves a unity that Chappell says is always at the heart of his work: "I aim for a unified effect on the reader, tone, theme, attitude." There also is music in Chappell's writing, not surprising given his love of music and its presence in his life. Chappell is also a fine cook who has written of the influence Julia Child has had on him and of his discovery, through her, "that cooking was an art as satisfying as music or poetry."

38

PAT CONROY would do anything for you. Laugh, fall on the floor, probably even stand on his head. He is larger than life and up-front and personal in every way and in every thing he does. At his home on an out-of-the-way barrier island off the South Carolina coast, close to the setting of his six books, he greets the photographer with typical exuberance. He's excited because someone has just sent him a copy of the 1964 literary magazine from his freshman year at The Citadel, Conroy's love it–hate it alma mater. It contains his first published poem, an amusing bit of doggerel: "The dreams of youth are pleasant dreams, of women vintage and the sea. Last night I dreamt I was a dog, who found an upperclassmen tree." "I caught such hell for that," Conroy recalls. He still catches hell from the school and some of its supporters for critical novels such as *The Lords of Discipline* (1980), but he takes it in stride and returns each volley with gusto. Conroy, fifty-one, was born in Atlanta and grew up a military brat, spending many of his formative years in Lowcountry South Carolina, for which he has retained a profound affection. "I am a child of the marshes and the tides." One of the nation's most successful writers, who has fashioned five best-selling books—all turned into films— from autobiographical angst, he does his writing these days standing up at a special writing table given him by his publisher to help ease back pain. And, as always, he writes in longhand, spending as many hours each day at the task as possible, with only a short break for lunch. "My mother raised me to be a writer," he says. For all his success, which includes screenplays for two of his novels, he lives simply in a home that is comfortable without pretension, dresses casually (some would say inattentively), and spends many weeks away from home to see his children from two former marriages and meet the phenomenal demands for his time from admirers.

PATRICIA CORNWELL lives in a high-security world. The best-selling author of seven mystery novels, she has received threats on her life and encountered more than her share of overzealous admirers. Her homes in Richmond, Virginia, and Los Angeles are well-protected. And the offices of Cornwell Enterprises in suburban Richmond—where she directs everything from her own strong, controlling image to the design of her books, from product planning to film producing—are unobtrusive but quite secure. Inside the contemporary, stylish offices, with an aquarium near the front door, Cornwell oversees a staff of employees, handles telephone calls (one from evangelist Billy Graham), and still manages time to greet the photographer for an unhurried session. She offers to put on the highly polished black shoes she wore for four years as a volunteer police officer in Richmond ("I directed some traffic, lighted flares, things like that"), absorbing events and environments she would use later in her books. "I love research. It's much more fun than writing. It's important that I know just what I put my characters through. If I'm going to have them do something, I want to experience it myself." In pursuit of such experiences, she has done everything from hanging from a helicopter to scuba diving. Wearing an expensive watch she bought to celebrate a new book contract, she poses with an old Browning pistol in front of her on the desk ("I don't want to hold it in the picture") as she grips a carved cane she acquired at a folk-art center a few years ago. A native of Miami, a graduate of Davidson College in North Carolina, and a former newspaper reporter, she wrote her first book in 1983, a biography of Billy Graham's wife Ruth. Her first novel, *Postmortem* (1990), won an unprecedented five international awards. Like the six novels that followed, it focuses on the forensic flair of her fictional protagonist, Dr. Kay Scarpetta, Virginia's chief medical examiner. Cornwell herself spent years doing research in a medical examiner's office.

HARRY CREWS was born to tenant farmers in rural south Georgia, and his life growing up was hard, impoverished, and often brutal. "It was a world in which survival depended on raw courage, a courage born out of desperation and sustained by a lack of alternatives," he wrote in his gritty, gripping 1978 autobiography *A Childhood: The Biography of a Place.* When Crews—the first in his family to graduate from high school—writes about the poor and downtrodden, it is from a perspective he knows intimately, more intimately than most authors in the South. But the pain he is feeling when the photographer visited his secluded, hard-to-find home in a woodsy area near Gainesville, Florida, in late 1996 was of a different sort. It stemmed from a knee that was causing him to limp and to move about with unusual caution. He works in his writing room, which is also the living room, with his papers on a board on his lap and his words later transferred to the computer. When he's ready for the editing and revising process, he moves to a guest room. It is there that he reads to the photographer from a work in progress, clearly proud of his labor. He has quite a sense of humor, which will come as no surprise to his readers, who know that humor often is interspersed with intense violence in his writings. Crews, sixty-one, an ex-Marine, has written nineteen books, most recently the novel *The Mulching of America* (1995). His first novel, *The Gospel Singer,* appeared in 1968, the year he returned to his alma mater, the University of Florida, to take the teaching position he still holds. Always straightforward and honest, sometimes painfully so, in his conversations, Crews talks openly about his personal problems and future directions, leavening the words with an assured air and a penchant for wit.

GUY DAVENPORT has lived a life rich in scholarship and intellectual creative pursuits and not at all based on the acquisition of material goods. The story is told that within a few hours of being notified in the summer of 1990 that he had won a MacArthur Fellowship—an honor which bestowed $365,000 on its recipient—he went to the grocery to purchase a six-pack of Perrier. "I was feeling rich," he confessed. The life of the mind has proved exciting and stimulating for this productive writer of prize-winning short fiction, poetry, essays, and translations. Born in Anderson, South Carolina, he studied at Duke University, Merton College, Oxford, as a Rhodes Scholar, and Harvard University (where he earned a Ph.D.). In a writing career spanning four decades, he has written or translated twenty-seven books, including eight collections of stories, the most recent of which is *The Cardiff Team* (1996). Currently a professor of English at the University of Kentucky in Lexington, Davenport was collecting the mail from his mailbox when he greeted the photographer on a fall afternoon. Inside, after some coffee and a walk through the book-lined rooms, Davenport posed in an office on the first floor of the two-story home. It is one of several areas inside and behind the house which have served at one time or another as writing space. He explains that when he finishes writing a book, "I'm so tired that it seems there could be nothing left for me to write." Davenport, sixty-nine, has never courted attention and has followed a rigorous but simple discipline in his writing and personal life. He walks daily and has never owned a television set, once having called both cars and televisions "soul-destroying mechanisms."

JAMES DICKEY died in January 1997 at the age of seventy-three, less than five months after agreeing to be photographed for this book. Short of breath and finding movement difficult, he sat surrounded by stacks of books rising from the floor—and a plate of scrambled eggs quickly growing cold. His part-time housekeeper had brought the food, nourishment the distinguished poet and author first complained about and finally ignored. Dickey posed in the living room of his home in suburban Columbia, South Carolina, where he had lived since 1968 when he joined the University of South Carolina as poet-in-residence. A native of Atlanta, Dickey worked in advertising and did not publish his first book of poems until *Into the Stone* appeared in 1960 when he was thirty-seven. He won the National Book Award for Poetry for *Buckdancer's Choice* in 1966. His best-known book remains his first novel, *Deliverance* (1970), for which he wrote the screenplay; he later appeared in the film version, too. A man of enormous intellect and imposing physical stature and the subject of outrageous stories throughout his life ("Not all of them are true," he said laughingly), Dickey was hospitalized in the early 1990s with liver problems and in the final months of his life required oxygen periodically. "This way of living is not worth a damn," he said. But his mind remained undiminished to the end, and his conversation on the day he was photographed moved easily and discerningly from the photography of Cartier-Bresson to the poetry of Theodore Roethke to the music of Anton Bruckner. Caught in the power of his shared knowledge, it was easy that day to forget the one-time macho image, shrunken by more than one hundred pounds. Until his final hospitalization, Dickey greeted visitors enthusiastically, retaining a bond with his readers forged many years prior to his status as a literary elder statesman. He also continued to meet his popular writing class at the university, right up until a week before his death.

ELLEN DOUGLAS, whose real-life name is Josephine Haxton, was born in Natchez, a sixth-generation Mississippian, and now lives in Jackson. Twice holder of the Eudora Welty Chair at Millsaps College, she lives in a small, quiet home she purchased two years ago, less than five minutes from Miss Welty's. "Yes, that's a very reassuring thought," she says. Her output includes six novels, the first of which, *A Family's Affairs,* was published in 1962 when she was forty and made her a winner of a prestigious Houghton Mifflin Literary Fellowship. She has also written a commentary on Walker Percy's *The Last Gentleman,* a narrative account of the integration crisis at the University of Mississippi, and a children's book. She received her pseudonym at the time her first book appeared when an editor submitted the manuscript to the Houghton Mifflin competition. She took the name to protect her family from recognizing themselves in the work: "It was a way to separate the private from the public." She shows off the sunny writing space that greets her when she begins work in the mornings, usually around nine. She works for several hours, as inspiration and energy meet. She uses an old but still serviceable computer, explaining, "I've never been a good typist. It's so much easier to strike the computer keys." Douglas, seventy-five, posed for the photographer near a tall secretary which she acquired from relatives by agreeing to hang a portrait of her stern-looking great-great-grandfather John Henderson in her home. In her books she has sought to discover the truth beneath the surface, examining traditional Southern fictional materials—the relations between blacks and whites and between families, the presence of the past in the present—through modern sensibilities. With her perception and talent, she has been compared to the best of the writers of twentieth-century Southern literature: William Faulkner, Eudora Welty, Peter Taylor, and Katherine Anne Porter.

JOHN DUFRESNE has gotten his share of rejection slips, but none quite like the outrageously humorous ones he writes about in his novel *Love Warps the Mind a Little*. "I know the feeling a writer gets with one of those, and you can try to dismiss it, or get angry. One way or another, you usually react," he says. Dufresne, forty-eight, would seem to have followed a successful path. His first book, a collection of stories entitled *The Way That Water Enters Stone*, was published in 1991 to high and unanimous praise. His first novel, *Louisiana Power and Light*, was released in 1994, followed three years later by his second, *Love Warps the Mind*. "I'm writing at a pace that's comfortable," he explains. He grew up in Worcester, Massachusetts, went to Worcester State College, and spent nearly seven years as a social worker in crisis prevention programs. But his jobs also included, he says, everything from driving cabs to picking blueberries to painting homes. "The best thing I did was decide to go to graduate school at the University of Arkansas," Dufresne says. That launched him on a writing career. He taught at several colleges around the South and spent three years in Monroe, Louisiana, the setting for his first novel. For the last seven years he's been living in South Florida with his wife and son, teaching writing at Florida International University for six of those years. He was photographed during a book tour to New Orleans in early 1997, standing near the exterior of the Faulkner House bookstore—an appropriate spot for a writer whose work has drawn comparison with the Nobel laureate. He explained that his writing regimen means that "I do a lot of sitting doing nothing at the kitchen table." He writes in the mornings, in longhand, with reference books and a hot cup of coffee always close by. He also finds the time to read the morning paper and help get his eleven-year-old son off to school. "I'm disciplined when I'm writing at home, but then I'm doing what I really enjoy doing. I'm not disciplined at all when I'm on tour like this, though," he laughs.

CLYDE EDGERTON kicks back, removes his shoes and socks, puts his bare feet on the table, plops the computer keyboard in his lap, and begins the day's work. He's writing in the tiny, cramped, windowless basement office he rented seven years ago when "Neither Susan [his wife] nor I had day jobs, and we spent too much time talking and drinking." It's only a few minutes from downtown Durham, North Carolina, the city of his birth, and fits him perfectly: "I needed a space without windows so I could concentrate on my writing. . . . There's a place to eat above me, there's a post office, a nice place to walk, a bookstore. Everything I need." On the otherwise bare door is a sign reading "Dusty's Air Taxi," and Edgerton has cards he hands out bearing that logo, recalling his aviation past, his experiences as a fighter pilot with the U.S. Air Force in Laos and Vietnam. He hasn't flown much lately, however, not since the crash several years ago of a small one-engine plane he piloted. He keeps a photograph of the plane in the office, "the way it used to look." Edgerton, fifty-two, published his first novel, *Raney,* in 1985 and has written five others, most recently *Redeye* in 1995. All of the novels have rural North Carolina settings with compelling, often offbeat characters, social satires centering around family relationships, and plots enriched by Edgerton's keen ear for dialect and insistent comic tone. He and his wife are also fine musicians and frequently perform together with other North Carolina authors (including Lee Smith) as the Tar Water Band. Edgerton is among the most entertaining of authors in his speaking engagements, expert in conveying the dialects and excruciating situations of his amusing characters.

PERCIVAL EVERETT grew up in Columbia, South Carolina, but has spent nearly all of his writing life away from the South. He has taught at the Universities of Wyoming and Kentucky, at Notre Dame, and at the University of California at Riverside, where he currently is a professor of English, directs the creative writing program, and finds time to travel to good fly-fishing locations. He's lived throughout the U.S., from Cape Cod to Portland, Oregon, and held a variety of jobs, including musician and sheep-ranch hand. Everett, thirty-nine, has written one shy of a dozen novels and books of short fiction to growing acclaim, incorporating styles ranging from realism to fabulism in works of comic fiction, science fiction, and even a book for children. Many of his works have a dark, angry edge, though it's usually tempered by a sharp wit. His photographs often project that harsh image. "Why do I look angry on my book jackets? I'm a black man in America. Why not be angry?" But in the same breath, he smiles— his sense of humor never disappears for long—and adds, "Actually, I see many more amusing things now, in my life and my writing." Writing, he says, is painful for him, "like going into a bad marriage, but you go ahead anyway because that's all you can do." Since his first books, beginning in 1983 with *Suder*, the story of a black third baseman for the Seattle Mariners, Everett has had his work published by small, regional publishers. "I'm not interested in selling a lot of books. I'm not a commercial writer. I do care about the importance of smaller publishers because they allow me to be involved with my books in every way." He lives with his wife Chessie, an artist, and has had several shows of his own paintings.

SHELBY FOOTE, despairing, wrote to his old friend Walker Percy in 1974, soon after the release of the last book in Foote's three-volume history of the Civil War: "Who the hell wants to read anything about the goddam Civil War?" It turns out almost everyone did—especially if Foote was writing—or talking—about it. The publication of his epic *The Civil War: A Narrative* and, more recently, his acclaimed appearances on Ken Burns's television documentary on the war gave Foote a fame he had never experienced as a novelist. "It is something I have had to learn to bear," he says with practiced courtliness. Foote, with his distinctive baritonal voice and stately appearance belying his age (soon to be eighty), graciously consented to meet the photographer at the author's suburban Memphis home on a hot August afternoon. His office, above the garage at the brick two-story residence, is reached by an exterior staircase. Inside is a long, elegant room with a fireplace and a bed. At his desk Foote writes in longhand with a dip pen, a style that is old-fashioned but eminently suited to him. Once that step is completed, the sentences are copied on an old manual typewriter. On the shelves above the desk are rows of leather bindings which hold his original handwritten manuscripts. His trilogy came to more than 1.2 million words: "Never thought I'd turn out to be windier than Gibbon," he once wrote to Percy. Born in Greenville, Mississippi, Foote published his first of six novels, *Tournament,* in 1949, followed by four others in the space of five years. He then took twenty years to finish the Civil War trilogy, referring to the project as "this iliad," before returning to fiction with the novel *September, September* in 1977. He continues to struggle with a long novel titled "Two Gates to the City" on which he has worked sporadically for nearly three decades.

RICHARD FORD was intently at work on what proved to be his Pulitzer Prize–winning novel *Independence Day* when the photographer arrived at his home in late 1994. On the wall behind him were postcards with scenes of Cooperstown, New York, the setting for part of the novel. "I was working feverishly to finish those segments of the book then. The postcard photographs were to help jog my memory a little, although they're really for atmosphere. Sometimes the photos can be so specific that they get in the way of my writing," he recalled. Ford, fifty-two, a native of Jackson, Mississippi, has written five novels and a collection of short stories (*Rock Springs*, 1987). His first novel, *A Piece of My Heart*, published in 1976, is the only one to date set in a Southern landscape. His second novel, *The Ultimate Good Luck*, appeared in 1981 and was followed five years later by *The Sportswriter*, his best-known novel before publication of its sequel, *Independence Day*. Ford has said of *The Sportswriter*, "I meant it as a plain-spoken, good-tempered book, serious about most of the things I'm serious about: making myself happy and cordial to the world, not fighting what can't be fought, fighting what can be, and letting a lot just go by without notice." Ford does his writing on a "graduated" schedule. "The work gets increasingly intense as I get closer to the end. When I start, I'm writing four or five hours a day. By the middle part of the book, I've usually found my own rhythm, and when I get to the stage when the photograph was made, I was working fifteen hours a day." He has written his manuscripts in pencil and now uses an inexpensive pen: "I like to see the ink deplete in the pen. It gives me great satisfaction, a sense of accomplishment," he laughs. He and his wife Kristina have lived in many locales, including Montana, California, Vermont, and Mexico, and their home now is in New Orleans, where Ford is a full-time writer.

CONNIE MAY FOWLER lets the truth slip out gracefully: she's not really a native of Florida as biographies on her book jackets proclaim. "I was conceived in St. Augustine, but I was actually born in Raleigh, N.C." She has spent almost her entire life in the Sunshine State, however, and now lives with her husband Mika in a beach house in Alligator Point near the Gulf waters. The locale's name is reinforced by the sight of gators dangling from her earlobes as she sits for the photographer in Nashville. She came to the Tennessee capital for the 1996 Southern Festival of Books to accept an award from the Southern Book Critics Circle for writing the best fiction of the year, *Before Women Had Wings,* her third of three novels, all published within five years. "This kind of success at my age [thirty-seven] is hard to believe. It's like the real Connie is sitting here by the water and hearing this wonderful news about someone else." Her lovely china-doll appearance is inviting but may deceive some about her inner strength and cloaks an often difficult past. She calls herself a survivor, triumphing over family problems that began with near poverty after the death of her father. Those sensitive issues she has transmuted into magical literary truth and triumph in her books. At the same time she has overcome a terrible problem with stuttering which once made her difficult to understand. "This is the best part of my life, right now," she says.

JOHN HOPE FRANKLIN, one of America's most distinguished historians, has been crazy about orchids for a long time. "Ever since 1959, when I was at the University of Hawaii," he recalls. The greenhouse at the rear of his warm, brick home in suburban Durham, North Carolina, attests to his knowledgeable affection over the years. The greenhouse—damaged when Hurricane Fran struck the heart of North Carolina a week before the photographer arrived—boasts multihued varieties, including one very special to the historian: the John Hope Franklin Orchid, named to recognize his passion for growing the flower. This award is one Franklin, a spry eighty-one, proudly discusses. He is more modest about the others, which include the Presidential Medal of Freedom, the nation's highest civilian award, given to him by President Clinton in 1995 and now resting on a table in his living room. Franklin, born in Oklahoma, earned his doctorate from Harvard and taught in the 1940s at North Carolina College for Negroes in Durham, then went on to Cambridge University in England and then to the University of Chicago before returning to Durham and Duke University. His 1947 study of African Americans, *From Slavery to Freedom,* remains in print in a seventh edition, and *Reconstruction and the Civil War* (1961) continues as a landmark account of that tumultuous period. Those books were written on a typewriter, but Franklin now has "fully embraced" the computer. He writes his lectures and speeches on it, as he was doing on the day he met the photographer, preparing to accept an award as Historian of the Century from former Duke president Terry Sanford. "He and I have been co-conspirators in planning a perfect society," Franklin said. "Now if the rest of the world would just follow."

ERNEST J. GAINES was photographed in 1993 at his home in Lafayette, Louisiana. He divides his time between San Francisco and that small college town where he has been writer-in-residence at the University of Southwest Louisiana for more than a decade. His continued presence at that out-of-the-mainstream campus has surprised some. But given his strong feelings of loyalty, it shouldn't be surprising. Following the release of the enormously popular television movie *The Autobiography of Miss Jane Pittman,* based on his 1971 novel, he began looking for a place to settle. He found that Southwest Louisiana was the only university willing to offer him a tenured position. He took it and vowed loyalty to the school—in spite of offers that have flowed to him from high-profile institutions in later years. Gaines, sixty-three, was born on a plantation near New Roads, Louisiana. The eldest of eleven siblings, he recalls going to work in the fields at the age of nine. His parents separated when he was a child, and he was raised by an aunt to whom he dedicated *Miss Jane Pittman* and who was the model for the fictional title character. Although he has lived for many years in California, his home state and his upbringing there have always been the core influences of his writing. He did some writing as a teenager and got a degree at San Francisco State College, but his literary career got its biggest boost when he won a Wallace Stegner Creative Writing Fellowship at Stanford University in 1958. His first book, the novel *Catherine Carmier,* was published in 1964, and he wrote two more books before *Miss Jane Pittman* won him widespread acclaim. His 1983 novel, *A Gathering of Old Men,* has a rural setting and tells the story of a group of old men guarding a secret. The men on whom he based the book may be glimpsed in the photograph next to the author. His most recent novel, *A Lesson Before Dying* (1993), won the Southern Book Critics Circle Award for the best work of fiction of the year.

GEORGE GARRETT greets the photographer three days after undergoing surgery to remove cataracts, explaining, "I've had twenty-four hours of the worst pain I've ever had." That's one of the few things that can slow down the peripatetic sixty-seven-year-old Florida-born writer. With his gregarious sensibilities, larger-than-life sense of humor, and uncanny recall of stories about writers and writing, he is unquestionably the most popular author in America's literary community. On average, he's traveling at least once a week from his home in Charlottesville, Virginia, to take part in workshops, seminars, and other academic programs, which call him insistently and regularly. "I just try to keep ahead of the American Express bill," Garrett says. The prolific author of twenty-five books—novels, short stories, essays, and poetry—and editor of nineteen others, he has always drafted his prose and poetry in longhand on legal-size pads. His wife Susan transcribes the words on the computer. He has an upstairs office at his home, but because it is so crowded with books and journals and research materials, he sometimes has to adjourn to the dining room table to compose. A few minutes away from the stone house where he has lived for over a decade is the famed Rotunda at the University of Virginia, where he is Hoyns Professor of Creative Writing. There he dispenses both pragmatic advice and discerning encouragement to students, dozens of whom have gone on to publication. His writing is often satiric and reflects his interest in social criticism. His first work appeared in 1957 in a volume of poetry, and his most recent is *The King of Babylon Shall Not Come Against You* (1996), a tragicomic story set in Florida during the week of the assassination of Dr. Martin Luther King, Jr.

KAYE GIBBONS was still in shock, suffering, like thousands of North Carolinians, from disbelief and dismay at the widespread destruction wreaked by Hurricane Fran, when she first met the photographer. They talked on the front porch of her home in suburban Raleigh where, just over one week before, the hurricane had arrived unexpectedly as it roared through the heart of the state. A large tree was uprooted and overturned in her front yard. Power had been lost for the entire week. Flooding and humidity had damaged books and photographs. She was casually attired in her usual writing outfit—jeans and a T-shirt "with cat hair all over it"—but nonetheless agreed to pose. "The hurricane will make it easier for me to write about what devastation means," she said with a menagerie of adopted cats and dogs (including a one-eyed poodle) scurrying about her feet. Under calmer circumstances a few months later at the Tennessee Williams Festival in New Orleans, she posed again for this photograph with a smile far removed from the post-hurricane days. The thirty-six-year-old native North Carolinian has struggled with family loss and, for more than a decade, manic-depression. The stability she requires is supplied, she says, by her supportive husband Frank and her three children. She also has had to adjust to the demands of satisfying a large and growing number of admirers of her five novels. The first one, *Ellen Foster,* appeared in 1987 and was honored with the Sue Kaufman Prize from the American Academy and Institute of Arts and Letters.

GAIL GODWIN enjoys a magnificent view of scenic, snow-covered woods from her home on the side of a hill. The lovely tract of about fifteen acres of land near Woodstock, New York, where she lives with her husband, the composer Robert Starer, offers a tranquillity appropriate to serious writing. It also offers an indoor swimming pool where Godwin exercises and relaxes each day. She extends a warm greeting to the photographer and escorts him upstairs to the office where she does her writing, sometimes with a little burning incense to help establish a particular atmosphere: "It can help to focus, to turn on the senses." Now fifty-nine, Godwin poses standing in her office, where she writes the first drafts of her manuscripts in longhand. She was born in Birmingham, Alabama, but her parents soon divorced, and her mother moved to Asheville, North Carolina, where Godwin grew up. She worked briefly as a newspaper reporter for the *Miami Herald* before turning to academic life and full-time writing. A creative writing class in London helped direct her, though writing seemed always foremost in her life. She wrote a novel while she was still in her teens, and in college she rewrote a novel her mother had written but abandoned. Most of Godwin's work has carried autobiographical connections, beginning with *The Perfectionists* in 1970, a first novel whose jacket, oddly, provided no biographical information about the author for the benefit of readers. She has written nine novels—most recently *The Good Husband* (1994)—and two collections of short stories, *Dream Children* (1976) and *Mr. Bedford and the Muses* (1983). Her work has been hailed for its compassion and intelligence and for her skill in narrative and creating strong feminine characters.

SHIRLEY ANN GRAU loves fishing. She's apologetic about missing an appointment, but the fish are biting and she hasn't been out to the Gulf coast for a while. It's fun and a wonderful way to relax for the Pulitzer-Prize–winning author who was born in New Orleans in 1929 and, except for a portion of her childhood in Alabama, has been close to the city all of her life. She has published short stories in several national magazines, including the *Saturday Evening Post* and the *Atlantic Monthly.* Her first published book, a collection of short stories, *The Black Prince,* was a sensation when it appeared in 1954, selling out its first printing in two weeks and winning for its author comparisons to Chekhov, Welty, and Capote. Two books later, she published her second novel, *The Keepers of the House* (1964), a thoughtful and perceptive examination of racial tensions in the Deep South, written on a mythic, even tragic scale. She received a Pulitzer for that book, becoming the youngest (at thirty-five) of the fifteen women recipients of the prize at the time. Only one of her books, *Evidence of Love* (1977), has a landscape outside of the South, and her newest, *Roadwalkers* (1994), is an eloquent novel about the lives of two black women in the rural South. Grau lives in a Bahaus home in the New Orleans suburb of Metairie, where she met the photographer with a warm greeting in late 1994. Her writing space is in the front of the house, a computer placed on an oval desk sometimes occupied by her cat. The desk is the only place she works now, she says, "because I travel so much, and when I do, I just can't do any writing." That wasn't always the case. She raised four children and became accustomed to writing when she could, whether during car pool breaks or at Little League baseball games. "The house was always a tangle of children's toys, clothes, animals, thousands of books," she once said, "and as is the case with most Southerners, is always full of visitors." On the jacket of her first book she declared her ambition to write "an even dozen novels." Grau now has published nine books, six of them novels, in a literary career spanning five decades.

JIM GRIMSLEY laughs about being "playwright-in-residence" at his small basement apartment in Atlanta's bohemian Little Five Points area. That's because his landlord also owns the 7Stages theater where Grimsley's prize-winning plays have been produced and where he is "officially" the playwright-in-residence. "It's a very nice arrangement," he explains. Grimsley also has a comfortable arrangement with Grady Hospital, where he works as an administrative secretary, a job that allows him flexibility to write and to complete publicity tours for his books. Grimsley, forty-one, was preparing to go on the road for his third novel, *My Drowning* (1997), when he met the photographer at the apartment in December. He posed in a reading chair with his twelve-year-old cat named Dingus ("I just made up the name") at his side. Grimsley does much of his writing in the evening hours after work, using a computer "because it's neater and I'm a neatness freak." Born in Rocky Mount, North Carolina, Grimsley went to UNC and studied writing with Doris Betts and Max Steele, at first producing science-fiction stories before looking to other subjects. He finished his first novel, *Winter Birds,* in 1984 but couldn't find an agent or publisher. Through friends, he made connections with a German publisher, and the novel first appeared there and in France before it was released in the United States in 1994. Grimsley's second novel, *Dream Boy,* was published just one year later. Grimsley is a hemophiliac and is HIV positive, calling himself "a fifteen-year HIV survivor." He proudly proclaims himself a gay writer and a Southern writer and answers questions about how long he expects to live by saying, "I plan to live to be 100. I don't feel at all mortal."

WINSTON GROOM found success with a fool. But what a fool. When his 1986 novel *Forrest Gump* became an Oscar-winning film in 1993 with actor Tom Hanks as the memorable title character, Groom became a household name. "Seven years late," he says. Even with that success, Groom, fifty-three, remains accessible and approachable, welcoming the photographer with good humor to his Point Clear, Alabama, home in early 1997. It's a new home, but it incorporates some key elements from the past. The front door, for instance, comes from an old hotel in Mobile. Groom works in an office on the ground floor of the two-story house, writing on a computer, up to two thousand words a day "when I'm clicking." In the office is a large poster for the film signed by each member of the cast. The 6'6" Groom was born in Washington, D.C., quite by accident, and lived for a while in Virginia. "I suppose my obituary will read I was born in Washington, but I've been in Alabama just about all of my life." At the age of eight he won an essay competition sponsored by the Mobile newspaper, receiving as a prize a book of Grimm's fairy tales, "And I've been stealing from it ever since." He was graduated from the University of Alabama and, like Gump, served in Vietnam. He was a captain in the 4th Infantry Division, and his first novel, *Better Times Than These* (1978), was set in Vietnam. He has written nine books, both fiction and nonfiction; his most recent nonfiction work, *Shrouds of Glory* (1995), is about the final Civil War campaign in Tennessee. *Forrest Gump* sold a respectable thirty thousand copies, but since the release of the film sales have surpassed 1.5 million. He produced a sequel, *Gump & Co.*, in 1995 but vows "there will not be a *Gump 5* or *6*."

ALLAN GURGANUS is restoring an old home he purchased a couple of years before in the town of Hillsborough, North Carolina, not far from Durham and Chapel Hill. The house was known at one time for being haunted, he explains, though the interior now reflects only the keen imagination and inspired, flamboyant decorating sensibilities of its owner. One space with columns Gurganus calls "My Pompeii room." As he shows the photographer around what must surely be the most exotic interior in Hillsborough, Gurganus is attired as eclectically as usual: velvet blazer, baggy pants, and red sneakers. "This wonderful watch fob belonged to my great-uncle," he says. His writing space includes a computer in a huge room with stained-glass windows, salmon-colored walls, and a bust of Thomas Jefferson. Upstairs is a bathroom done in black and white with a copper ceiling, a bank of aisle lighting, and a large window by the oversized tub. It is by any measure a remarkable room in a remarkable home. "One lives at the brink of self-caricature," Gurganus, forty-nine, says. Born in Rocky Mount, North Carolina, he served in Vietnam, studied writing with the likes of John Cheever, Stanley Elkin, and Grace Paley, and burst onto the literary scene in 1989 with his novel *Oldest Living Confederate Widow Tells All.* In that book he created one of literature's most striking characters, ninety-nine-year-old Lucy Mardsen, who recounts her life from marriage at the age of fifteen to a much-older Confederate veteran to her days in a nursing home. Gurganus, whose second book, *White People,* a collection of stories, was published in 1991, used to write his manuscripts in longhand but now concedes the primacy of the computer. "I write six days a week, and when I start I don't stop for anything. I won't even take calls until late afternoon when I finish for the day."

BARRY HANNAH, wearing tennis shorts, strolled into Square Books in downtown Oxford, Mississippi, on a lovely, warm fall morning and asked if anyone had seen the photographer. "C'mon, let's go to the house," he said. There, he proudly showed his writing space off the back of the main house and posed for a photograph—until he was called out on an errand. The session was suspended for an hour until Hannah returned, picking up exactly where he had left off. The tennis clothing is no affectation: it's part of the fifty-four-year-old author's exercise and diet regimen in recent years. "It's a real change of life for me. And I'm not kidding you, it's got me feeling better than I have in a long time. And I haven't had a drink in seven years." He also is on the tennis court three times a week, playing intensely and competitively. A native of Meridian, Mississippi, Hannah has used the region around his hometown in much of his fiction over the years. An occasional writer of poetry, he turned to fiction while teaching at Clemson University, and it was there that he completed his first novel, *Geronimo Rex,* published in 1972. Harry Crews called it "a lyrical, half-crazed song about growing up in the South," and it won the William Faulkner Prize. Hannah has written eleven works of fiction, daring and original, most recently a short-story collection, *High Lonesome* (1996). Like many of his other books, it has a darkly comic vision and a landscape marked sometimes by violence and sometimes by humor. Hannah has been writer-in-residence at the University of Mississippi for the last decade.

CARL HIAASEN grew up around Fort Lauderdale. "And back then there weren't many kids around to play with. But there were lots of snakes, so I started playing with them." Now he's interested in some of the environmentally endangered species. At his recently purchased home in the Florida Keys, for instance, he's taking care of an albino corn snake with a ravenous appetite for mice. Hiaasen's passion for the natural environment—and his belief in the fact that developers and politicians have corrupted it—is evident throughout the six novels he has written over the last decade. These wildly comic crime novels, with an underpinning of anger, portray the craziness of South Florida with a cast of characters including a stripper with a heart of gold, greed-driven politicians, murderous plastic surgeons, reptile smugglers, and conniving roofers gouging hurricane-struck Miamians. "I do worry a lot about what's happened to Florida," Hiaasen, forty-four, says. "One of the reasons I came to the Keys is because this is one of the few places left worth saving." He's been in Florida all his life, leaving only for a couple of years to attend Emory University in Atlanta. Hiaasen has been an investigative reporter and columnist for the *Miami Herald* for more than twenty years. In the real world, he seldom sees justice done, but he evens the score in his books: "In a novel you can extract a sense of justice. . . . Most things don't have a happy ending. I can make that happen in my novels, though." He wrote three novels with a colleague at the newspaper before publishing his first by himself, *Tourist Season* (1986). His home boasts a beautiful view of Florida Bay, but his writing space has no windows facing the water: "It's too distracting otherwise." The room does display a poster of actress Demi Moore, inscribed to Hiaasen who wrote the novel *Strip Tease* on which her film was based. On a good day, he writes upward of a thousand words. And when he's not writing, he says with a smile, he's probably out fishing.

JOSEPHINE HUMPHREYS arrives early, sometimes by 4:30 A.M., at the Confederate Home, a historic building in the heart of historic Charleston, South Carolina. There, occasionally comforted by a cappuccino obtained from a nearby all-night service station, she begins her day of writing novels that sensitively and perceptively explore the fragility of contemporary relationships. Her roomy warren was, in an earlier time, an apartment given over to the aging women who had been married to survivors of the Civil War in a city where the first guns of battle in that war were heard. There Humphreys practices her secret vice (smoking) and writes, sitting in a comfortable chair in a corner with a computer keyboard placed on a breakfast tray, then transferred to her lap. "The chair is the one place I've found that doesn't hurt my back." Humphreys's piercing blue eyes are behind a pair of reading glasses when she writes, and at least a half dozen pairs of glasses are scattered about so that there'll always be one on hand. In one corner is a telephone with an answering machine to fend off callers when she's busy. In another, a lighted lava lamp, a relic of the 1960s, churns away, much to the amusement of the author. The soft-spoken fifty-one-year-old Humphreys, mother of two college-age boys and a self-described "social recluse," lives with her attorney husband in a beachfront home near Charleston. A native of the city who went away to Duke and Yale for her education and published her PEN/Faulkner Award-winning first novel *Dreams of Sleep* in 1984, Humphreys fits with growing, graceful ease into the traditions of this heritage-heavy coastal city.

JOHN JAKES was born in Ohio and has split his life between Connecticut and South Carolina for two decades, but he has chosen to become a Southerner by residence in the last ten years since he built a home at Hilton Head Island, along the lower South Carolina coast. His orientation was confirmed two years ago when his adopted state inducted him into its literary hall of fame, joining the likes of William Gilmore Simms, DuBose Heyward, Julia Peterkin, James Dickey, and Pat Conroy. "We're very happy here, and as I get older, this becomes more and more our permanent address. I think we'll sell the Connecticut home," says the sixty-four-year-old author of at least sixty-five books published since 1952. Jakes's home, with many postcard views of the quiet waters of Calibogue Sound from its large glass windows, reflects comfort and contentment. But how does he manage to spend any time writing in his bookshelf-heavy second-floor office with such a distracting view? "I keep the computer on the other side of the room so I have to face away," he says with a smile. Jakes is a professional writer; he doesn't teach, nor does he hold other jobs. He goes to his office at 8 A.M. each day and writes on his computer until at least noon, sometimes as late as dinner time. "Writing is a craft. You have to work at it." Jakes long has been one of the champions of the nation's libraries, which have welcomed him for the voluminous and intensive research required for his best-selling historical novels such as *North and South* (1982) and his latest novel, *Homeland* (1993). Jakes worked in advertising for seventeen years before becoming a full-time writer, but that's not the only change in his life. He recently dropped more than fifty pounds after having a minor heart attack. "I took that very seriously. And the recovery, at least it gave me some time to catch up on some of my reading."

ROBERT JORDAN isn't his real name. Nor is Reagan O'Neal, Jackson O'Reilly, or Chang Lung. They're all pseudonyms James O. Rigney, Jr., of Charleston, South Carolina, has used in writing nearly two dozen widely read books. Robert Jordan has been his most popular name, however, and in that guise he has written seven heroic fantasy novels in the Conan series and seven more in a high fantasy series called The Wheel of Time which has over five million copies in print. The most recent novel in that series, *A Crown of Swords,* was the nation's number one best-seller for a time in the summer of 1996. A native of the city where he now lives and works, Jordan, forty-nine, taught himself to read at the age of four and at one time was reading four hundred books a year. He served two tours of duty in Vietnam, earning the Distinguished Flying Cross and the Bronze Star. He received a degree in physics from The Citadel and went to work as a nuclear engineer but turned to writing historical fiction while recuperating from an injury. He met the photographer in early 1997 at the spectacular two-hundred-year-old home where he and his wife Harriet live in Charleston's most historic section. He conversed easily on topics as diverse as politics and literacy while sitting in the living room, sipping tea, and smoking one of the dozens of pipes in his collection. The use of pseudonyms—different names for different types of books—helps him maintain control and privacy. He does not care to have his real name used on his writing, has an unlisted telephone number, and requests that his address not be given out, all to minimize interruptions from well-meaning but overeager fans. Jordan, who once wrote a western novel in just thirteen days, doesn't mind hard work and takes his writing very seriously: "I write seven days a week, no days off last year and most of the year before. In fact, my publisher told me I ought to take some time off. Can you imagine a publisher telling a writer to take time off?" When he's at the computer, "I'm running on adrenaline and coffee. I can't get my brain to slow down. I'm the most laid-back Type A personality you've ever seen."

TERRY KAY likes to write in cheap motels. In fact, he does his best work there. "I'm an old newspaperman, and I've always worked best under a tight deadline," he explains to the photographer. "So I go and rent a motel room for a week, bring in the cooler and a coffee maker and start writing." He tries to write for about four hours at a time, then nap or eat, and start over again. "I don't need great views out the window, and I don't turn on the TV." To have his picture made, he went to the photographer's motel near the Fulton County airport in Atlanta ("This is cheap enough for me. I've stayed here before," Kay said) and brought out the portable computer he uses for his writing. "This room is great; it's so small you can roll from the chair to the bed without even bothering to stand up." Kay grew up on a forty-acre farm in Hart County, Georgia, near the birthplace of baseball legend Ty Cobb. The eleventh of twelve children, he went to school in Georgia and started work as a journalist in the state in 1959. For eight years he was theater and film reviewer for the *Atlanta Journal.* His first book, the novel *The Year the Lights Came On,* was published in 1976, soon after he left the newspaper job. "I started going to motels when I was trying to write that book because my wife told me to 'Get out.' I did find a way to write without distractions," he says with a laugh. That novel, a loosely autobiographical reminiscence about the coming of electricity in a rural area of Georgia in 1947, has been followed by five books, most recently the novel *Shadow Song* (1994). He also was the author of the Emmy Award–winning screenplay *Run Down the Rabbit.* Kay proudly confirms his status as a Southern writer, adding, "The best writing has always come from the South."

BRET LOTT grew up in California, went to school in the Northeast, and didn't come South until 1986, when he became the first writer-in-residence at the College of Charleston. Getting his first glimpse of the city, with its lushness and semitropical heat, he remarked, "It looks like Pirateland at Disney World." A decade later, it is home, and Lott professes to be very comfortable and honored at being firmly placed now as a writer of the South. Deeply religious, Lott and his wife Melanie ("She's my best critic.") home-school their two boys, with the 6'3" Lott taking the role of the principal: "I can be very intimidating." He still teaches at the college, takes part in numerous seminars and workshops for writer wannabes, and does his own writing in an upstairs room at their new two-story suburban home. There he has produced four novels and two books of stories with a spare, poignant prose style that has won critical praise and comparisons to the late Raymond Carver. "The story is what counts; no tricks, no gimmicks. If the story is clear to me, I think it will be clear for the reader," Lott says, sitting at his computer. His day begins before sunrise with the first of many cups of coffee (half decaf) in his writing room, cluttered with the familiar—children's clothes on the floor, the walls bearing jackets from his books and turkey feathers from a successful hunt in the Lowcountry a few years ago. He first apologizes for the disorder, then admits that his "inner sanctum" is really the one place where he is fully and completely a writer.

BOBBIE ANN MASON grew up on a farm in Western Kentucky where she pored over books in an oak grove. She graduated from the University of Kentucky and now lives in the state. "I don't mind the designation as a Kentucky writer, or as a Southern writer, as a geographical statement. But it can be limiting to some, and I don't write for a specific audience." Mason, fifty-six, isn't at home to have her photograph made, however. She's in Nashville during the 1996 Southern Festival of Books, and she has agreed to pose inside the Tennessee capitol building. A few steps away from the granite columns where she stands quietly is a statue of Tennessee native son Andrew Johnson, "who is not my favorite Andrew," Mason says laughingly. That would be Andrew Jackson, whose home The Hermitage is only a few miles away. "I've been doing some research into some of the records about my family who came from near there in Middle Tennessee." Mason's first book of fiction, *Shiloh and Other Stories,* appeared in 1982 after a pair of nonfiction studies, one of them devoted to the subject of Nancy Drew and other girl-sleuths she read enthusiastically in her youth. In her five books she has written with subtlety and compassion of ordinary people searching for truth and meaning in the dramatic changes in their lives and relationships in the post–Vietnam War era. Critics have compared her thematic concerns to those of Flannery O'Connor, Carson McCullers, and Allen Tate. For her novel *Feather Crowns* (1993) she received the Southern Book Critics Circle award for the best work of fiction for the year.

ED MCCLANAHAN didn't have far to go to sign copies of his latest book, *A Congress of Wonders,* when he met the photographer at Black Swan Books in Lexington, Kentucky, in mid-October. He was born in Brooksville, Kentucky, in 1932, but Lexington is now his hometown. It took a few minutes to make his photograph because so many friends and well-wishers showed up to get their books autographed. "Makes you feel pretty good," he said with a big smile. He wrote for his small-town high-school newspaper and expected to major in journalism. He started off at Washington and Lee University but got his undergraduate degree from Miami University in Ohio and a master's degree from the University of Kentucky. He taught at a number of schools and published many short stories, but his first book was a novel, *The Natural Man.* Published in 1983, it is a comic coming-of-age tale set in rural Kentucky in the 1940s which some critics have compared to books by J. D. Salinger and Mark Twain. "I'm a very slow writer," he says, and his second novel, *A Congress of Wonders,* which takes place in a carnival sideshow during World War II, was published thirteen years after his debut book. In between was a sort-of autobiography, an ironically titled nonfiction book of portraits of ordinary people McClanahan met during thirty years of wanderings, *Famous People I Have Known* (1985). McClanahan says he has irregular writing hours but is persistent about putting words to paper—or rather computer. "The only time I ever sat down and wrote a certain number of pages each day was when I was doing the first draft of *The Natural Man.* And I wrote that in a white heat," he said in a recent interview.

JILL MCCORKLE smiles when she gets around the campus of the University of North Carolina at Chapel Hill. The thirty-eight-year-old Lumberton, North Carolina, native got her degree from UNC and taught writing there before heading to Boston with her husband. "I miss this campus. I come back every chance I get," she said while posing at the famed Old Well on the historic campus. Exuding Southern charm and warmth, she worries about her appearance for the camera: "When I smile, my eyes get all squinty. Nobody can make a good picture of me." But she relaxes quickly and is off on a storytelling jaunt, losing self-consciousness faster than she could ever drop her pronounced eastern Tar Heel accent. When she was just twenty-five, she became one of the rare authors whose first two books of fiction, *The Cheerleader* and *July 7th,* were published simultaneously. McCorkle writes about characters faced with the necessity of growing up, a process she illuminates with the gift of finding laughter in unlikely situations. Since her debut she has written three novels, *Tending to Virginia* (1987), *Ferris Beach* (1990), and her latest, *Carolina Moon* (1996), a tale about illicit secrets in a small town. She also has completed one collection of short stories, *Crash Diet,* published in 1992. Though she lives away from North Carolina now, teaching at Harvard University and Bennington College, the settings of her books continue to be of her home state, and she remains part of the close-knit community of writers who congregate in the area of Chapel Hill, Raleigh, and Durham. "I couldn't imagine not being a part of North Carolina no matter where I am. It's like having a second skin you can't shed. Of course I don't want to shed," she adds with another vibrant laugh.

TIM MCLAURIN looks like at least forty miles of bad road this afternoon. He's tired. He was out partying the night before, and the effects haven't completely worn off. "Too many beers, you know." A cup of coffee is called for. Or maybe a snake. McLaurin knows all about them. He's been a snake handler in a carnival, he's used them to help teach youngsters about reptiles, and he's always had a few around the house. Like the python in a cage in the living room. It's not quite as threatening as the copperhead he picked up on the road whose savage bite still shows two years later in his disfigured finger. McLaurin, a native of Fayetteville, North Carolina, has lived in the Tar Heel State most of his life, except for his service with the Marines in Vietnam and with the Peace Corps in North Africa and for the months he spent in a veterans' hospital in Seattle battling—and defeating—a life-threatening multiple myeloma. He wrote his first novel, *The Acorn Plan,* in 1988 and has completed two others along with a nonfiction memoir of growing up in the South, *Keeper of the Moon* (1991). That memoir, he wrote, "is about whippings and birthing farm animals, that first cold beer, hunting, holidays, integration, snakes, soldiers, fevered young love, fights, drunkards and divorce." He teaches writing at North Carolina State University, a short ride in the pickup from his home near Raleigh. His gritty, tough prose style has been compared to that of Harry Crews, and he has leavened the anger of many of his characters with an ironic wit. Born in poverty, McLaurin, forty-two, has written about the poor and those out of society's mainstream, endowing them with an unromanticized dignity.

ROBERT MORGAN grew up on a farm in the Blue Ridge Mountains of North Carolina on land near Hendersonville settled two hundred years earlier by his Welsh ancestors. "I was born on the same day [October 3] as Thomas Wolfe," he says. He went to college expecting to major in science and mathematics, but a creative writing course under the late Guy Owens at North Carolina State University "changed my life." He later studied under Fred Chappell, another North Carolinian from the western mountains. At the age of twenty-six he went off to teach at Cornell University in Ithaca, New York, where he has been since 1971. He greeted the photographer at the door to his farm outside Ithaca on a snowy late-December afternoon and settled into the living room warmed by a brightly burning fireplace. "Living in New York gives me some distance. . . . I really became aware of being Southern only after I left North Carolina. There is a danger of romanticizing yourself and your writing if you go away, but I think I've resisted that." Morgan's writing routine involves rising before dawn, preparing coffee, and settling in a large, overstuffed chair to begin putting his thoughts into a spiral notebook. His first book, published in 1969, was *Zirconia Poems,* named for the community where his family lives in North Carolina and where zircons and zirconium have been mined since the nineteenth century. Known primarily for his poems—he has written nine books of poetry—Morgan came late to fiction. "There was an audience for poetry in the 1960s, but fiction is now more accessible," he says. He has produced four works of fiction, beginning in 1989 with a collection of stories, *The Blue Valleys,* and most recently the novel *The Truest Pleasure* (1995), in addition to completing a volume of nonfiction essays. Morgan writes with an eloquent, subtle, lyric touch and a strong sense of place, using the North Carolina mountains as the setting for many of his stories and poems.

WILLIE MORRIS got his introduction to one of the literary masters at an early age. He was eight when he accompanied his mother to the Jitney Jungle grocery in Jackson, Mississippi, and there, by the vegetable bin, he was introduced to Eudora Welty, who was in the store for her own morning shopping. He was born in Jackson but grew up in Yazoo City, a tiny town "on the edge of the Delta, straddling that memorable divide where the hills end and the flat land begins." He got his first writing job as a correspondent for the weekly paper in town, receiving a nickel an inch for his copy. He remembers one of his first published stories was about a local baseball game. His editor called him into the office and asked him to go cover another game, but this time, "Could you please try to get the final score somewhere in the story?" Morris, now sixty-two, absorbed the lesson and has gone on to a distinguished career as journalist, essayist, novelist, and editor. He was thirty-two when he arrived in New York City, eventually to become the youngest editor-in-chief at *Harper's*, America's oldest magazine. During his tenure (1967–71) he made the magazine, in the words of critic William Moss, "probably the most significant . . . in America," with contributions from some of the nation's best writers (including William Styron, James Dickey, and Robert Penn Warren). Soon after becoming the editor, he published his first book, *North Toward Home* (1967), a vivid, sometimes Thomas Wolfe–like autobiography that traced Morris's life from small-town Mississippi to the University of Texas, to Oxford as a Rhodes Scholar, and finally New York. His work has chronicled the timeless Southern issue of conflict between the insistence of memory and the need for change. Among his sixteen books are *Yazoo: Integration in a Deep-Southern Town* (1971), his first novel *The Last of the Southern Girls* (1973), and the sequel to *North Toward Home* published in 1993, the eloquent *New York Days*. Photographed at his home in Jackson, Morris does most of his writing in the afternoon, shunning the computer, writing his words in longhand on a pair of long tables in an upstairs writing room.

LAWRENCE NAUMOFF was born and raised in Charlotte, North Carolina, an "outsider," in his words, as the only male in a family of four sisters and a Jew in the predominately Christian South. In the 1960s he went to the University of North Carolina at Chapel Hill, where he won writing prizes and appeared to be headed for a major literary career. But it was two decades later, in 1988, when his first book, the comic novel *The Night of the Weeping Women,* was published. In the interim he was married twice, spent time in Mexico, returned to his native state, and bought a farm in the pre–Revolutionary War Quaker community of Silk Hope (which would give the title to his fourth and most recent novel in 1994). For ten years he lived in "a form of isolation" before gradually beginning to write again. Now, apparently comfortably settled near Chapel Hill and in a good relationship with "my longtime sweetheart," Marianne Gingher, another author, he writes with the passion, ironic eye, and originality so many predicted for him years before. A house builder and carpenter, he alternates working on houses with working on novels: "Dirty hands, clean senses," he says. He met the photographer and posed near a trailer home where he has been constructing a back porch for an elderly couple. There, and at jobs involving larger, expensive homes, he works gracefully with his hands in the act of creation. He proudly calls himself a "contrarian" for his sometimes contrary beliefs. His novels all have featured women who are much stronger than the men. "They are also, unlike the men, always victims of their own enthusiasm for life, victims of their own spiritedness," he wrote in a 1994 self-profile. And they are "most of all, victims of good-hearted wantonness, of the giving and taking of pleasure, which always seems, in my books, to force a heavy personal and cultural consequence."

LEWIS NORDAN posed for his photograph in the spring of 1997. The setting is Capitol Street, Jackson, Mississippi, at the Magnolia Restaurant, an establishment that opened in 1935 and one that he frequented when he was a student at Millsaps College some years back. "The decorations haven't changed a bit," he said with a laugh, "but the food is just as good." Nordan is all about Mississippi, though he hasn't been living in the state for the last fifteen years. He was born in Jackson and moved to the tiny Delta town of Itta Bena eighteen months later when his father died. He's been writing for much of his adult life, which includes acquiring a master's degree at Mississippi State University and a Ph.D. at Auburn. "I did a lot of really different things. I was an attendant to a quadriplegic, I sold fireworks, I was a high school teacher, a night watchman. Heck, I even reviewed books. I was doing anything I could because I couldn't get a job. I wanted to be a Shakespeare scholar, but I wasn't any good at that." He was successfully selling stories to magazines, however, and that led to his first book, a collection of Mississippi stories, *Welcome to the Arrow-Catcher Fair,* published in 1983. Three years later his second collection, *The All-Girl Football Team,* appeared, to growing acclaim. Now the author of seven books of fiction, Nordan has been hailed by fellow authors and readers as one of the finest writers of fiction in the United States, honored for his graceful imagination, buoyant wit, and technical authority. His novel *Wolf Whistle* (1993), a compelling look at racism based on a 1950s murder in Mississippi, was named best book of the year by the Southern Book Critics Circle. His most recent novel, *Lightning Song,* was published in the spring of 1997. Since 1983 he has been a professor of creative of writing at the University of Pittsburgh—a job and a city, he says, that "fit me perfectly."

110

PADGETT POWELL's first novel, *Edisto*, was named one of the five best books of fiction in the year of its publication, 1984. A decade later, he decided to write a sequel, *Edisto Revisited*, published in 1996. Why? "You write what is possible. Twisting and turning within your limitations," says the forty-four-year-old native of Gainesville, Florida. "I didn't start out to write a sequel. It was just there to be written." He grew up in various cities in South Carolina and went to the College of Charleston, arriving there, he says with a smile, "a ruined, dissolute pornographer. I was ready for dereliction." He was an English major because he thought that would help him write "until I figured out that was about as far away from a writer as I could get." He did absorb writing lessons there and also at graduate school, where he studied with Donald Barthelme. When *Edisto* was published, the late Walker Percy called it "sharper, funnier and more poignant than *Catcher in the Rye*." Two novels and one short-story collection later, Powell is back in Gainesville teaching at the University of Florida. The photographer found him at his home out in the country on a 180–acre tract jointly owned by Powell and several other people. He writes in a space upstairs in this two-story home, though he says he used to write anywhere he could: offices, coffee shops, any place. "As you get older, unfortunately, people think you're weird to be doing something like that." He manages to find time for his writing, though it can be difficult with two school-age daughters. In fact, he had to interrupt the photographer in mid-afternoon in order to leave the house and pick up the girls from school. When he returned the session continued. Powell prides himself on his literary independence. "You work indifferent to certain norms," he says. "Good writers write from vigorous indifference to those traditions."

REYNOLDS PRICE lives on a hill in a heavily wooded area only a few miles from the Duke University campus in Durham, North Carolina, where he has taught since 1959. One of America's most honored writers and the author of twenty-nine novels and books of short fiction, as well as essays, poetry, plays, and translations, beginning with the prize-winning novel *A Long and Happy Life* in 1961, Price has chosen to live and work in the state where he was born in 1933. His home, which he moved into in 1965, has been remodeled to conform to his present needs. Diagnosed with cancer of the spinal cord in 1984, Price—who charted his agonizing recovery in the eloquent memoir *A Whole New Life* in 1994—now requires a wheelchair and made an addition to the house to have his bedroom placed on the main floor. In spite of the heavy rain this afternoon, he is jovial and animated when he greets the photographer in a brick-lined room filled with paintings, sculptures, various artistic icons, and a harpsichord, all reflecting the author's eclectic interests. He makes jokes about how people will defer to "the cripple," as he calls himself with a laugh. "They come up to me and say, 'How are you? No, I mean how aaaarrre you?' It's funny, but it can be a little tiresome. The fact is I'm fine. I'm in a wheelchair, but look at me." In spite of some limits on his maneuverability, Price is more in demand as a speaker and reader than ever. He fends off most speaking invitations, however, "not because I can't but because I don't want to do it. I need to write." He again laughs about setting his fees "outrageously," and "if someone says fine, then off I go." Duke provides him with a graduate-student assistant who helps take care of him for a year, an arrangement which Price says is critical in helping him meet daily obligations. In the twenty-two years before he was diagnosed with cancer, Price produced twelve books. In the twelve years since, he has published fifteen more. "And I'm not through yet."

ANNE RICE is one of America's most successful writers and probably the best-known cult author in the world. Her books about vampires, mummies, and other creatures of the dark have fascinated millions of readers for more than two decades. She has made appearances at book signings carried aloft in a coffin. And among her seventeen books published since 1976 are a trio of erotic novels released between 1983 and 1985 under the pseudonym A. N. Roquelaure: *The Claiming of Sleeping Beauty, Beauty's Punishment,* and *Beauty's Release.* Rice also is one of the busiest, most prolific of authors, and it was difficult for her to find time to sit for the photographer. A bright, intense woman, she surrounds her writing space in her Garden District mansion in New Orleans with an eclectic mix of fantasy and reality. In front of her are the open pages of the Bible. "I read myself awake with it every morning," Rice says. Nearby are religious artifacts, dolls, a stuffed owl, and an Elvis figure. And words, hundreds of words, stored on her computer and even written on the walls. "When a title comes to me, I want to write it down with my Magic Marker anywhere I can," she says. Having run out of space in easily reached areas, she's had to bring a ladder up to her second-floor writing area to enable her to reach the upper parts of the walls. Rice, fifty-five, was born in New Orleans and given the name Howard Allen Frances O'Brien. She married the poet Stan Rice and lived in San Francisco before returning to the city of her birth. She was thirty-four when she sold her first book, the novel *Interview with the Vampire* (1976). Her novels since include *The Vampire Lestat* (1985), *The Queen of the Damned* (1988), *The Witching Hour* (1990), *Lasher* (1993), and, most recently, *Servant of the Bones* (1996), all ranking among the nation's best-selling books in the years they appeared.

LOUIS D. RUBIN, JR., arguably has taught more good writers than anyone in the United States. He's written, edited, and published more books about the literary life of the South than anyone else, too. With his pseudo-curmudgeonly demeanor and an ever-present pipe, he might seem a throwback to another, earlier literary era. The 1925 Underwood typewriter in the crowded office at the rear of his woodsy Chapel Hill, North Carolina, home reinforces the notion. "I wrote a lot of books on that," says the author and editor of some three dozen volumes. But Rubin, who grew up in Charleston, South Carolina, has a computer nearby, a 1994 Macintosh, and confesses that he utilizes the typewriter now only for envelopes. A former journalist, he learned and still uses the two-finger typing method. Behind the terminal is his worn, comfortable couch, now crowded with manuscripts but able quickly to be swept clean for a prone reading or the occasional nap. He is now retired after a distinguished lifetime of teaching at the Johns Hopkins University, Hollins College, and the University of North Carolina. The seventy-three-year-old Rubin also founded what became in less than a decade one of the South's premier publishers, Algonquin Books of Chapel Hill, which publishes the work of some of his finest former students. He has written a trio of novels beginning with *The Golden Weather* in 1961 and including *Surfaces of a Diamond* (1981) and *The Heat of the Sun* (1995), all with an affectionate and nostalgic nod to the South Carolina city where he grew up and which recently named him to its literary hall of fame.

FERROL SAMS at seventy-four is still a practicing physician in Fayetteville, Georgia, the town where he was born. The house in which he was born was built in 1848 and now is home to a sixth generation of the Sams clan. He's up before sunrise to get his writing done each day, and when the photographer arrived at his house at 7 A.M., Sams had finished writing and was doing some editing over a steaming cup of coffee in the kitchen. An hour later, and in spite of telephone calls to and from half a dozen patients and doctors, the manuscript was ready for typing—and Sams was off to the Fayette Medical Clinic one mile away to begin seeing the day's schedule of patients. "I'm a doctor taking care of people. That's my job," says Sams. "Writing is what I do because I have to." He's been a physician at the clinic since 1951, and his wife Helen and two of their four children practice there as well. A masterful storyteller with a puckish wit who can keep audiences laughing uproariously, Sams came to writing relatively late in his life. A graduate of Mercer University and the Emory University School of Medicine, he chose to draw his fiction from the events and people in his own life. His first novel, *Run with the Horsemen,* published in 1982 when he was sixty, recalled the simple ways of life in rural Georgia when adherence to behavioral codes was traditional and expected (and sometimes questioned by young people). With *Whisper of the River* (1984) and *When All the World Was Young* (1991), Sams completed his fictional trilogy, tracing the odyssey of young Porter Osborne, Jr., through adolescence into medical school and European adventures during World War II. Among Sams's six books are a pair of nonfiction works, *The Passing* and *Christmas Gift!*, which explores holiday traditions of an earlier generation.

DORI SANDERS is proud to call herself a farmer. She lived and worked on a farm before her literary success in her sixties, and now—the author of three books—a cookbook/storybook and two novels—she continues to work on the two-hundred-acre family peach farm in Filbert, South Carolina, where she grew up. While talking with the photographer, in fact, she stops to greet a customer driving up to the open-air roadside produce stand, long after the end of peach season: "We've got sweet potatoes and some turnips. The potatoes are good, robust, to die for. Hmmmm. Come back this afternoon, we'll have them for you." With her childlike, seemingly limitless reserves of energy and enthusiasm and a well of stories that never runs dry, she has become one of the most in-demand Southern authors since the release of her first novel, *Clover,* in 1990. She does most of her writing when it is not time to grow and sell peaches. At the stand, where she can most often be found when the summer heat is at its worst, she has constructed an addition with a brick floor she calls "The Front Porch," and there —while parents buy fresh produce—she entertains their youngsters with stories. "The mamas are buying and I'm talking and everything is just going great. That's the best." In the middle of the acreage is a large rock outcropping which she calls "Storytelling Rock" and has used in the past for talks with youngsters. She was born in York County, the eighth of ten children. Her father was a school principal and author, and she speaks of his love and his quiet courage in an era when rigid segregation was the norm. "I love to talk about him. And I love to talk about my fine peaches. Oh, you know, I just love to talk."

MARY LEE SETTLE is working on her next book when the photographer visits her home on a hillside with its majestic view of the snowy Blue Ridge near Charlottesville, Virginia, in the late fall. Spread out on a desk in her office is a copy of the newspaper from Charleston, West Virginia—where she was born—from the day of her birth in July 1918. It is one of the cues helping her assemble an autobiography, and behind her, on a wall, are old but newly restored black-and-white photographs of family, her mother, and her grandmother, Addie. "Discovering those pictures is how I could write an autobiography," she says. "We re-live our childhoods all the time." Settle embraced the computer more than a decade ago. "I used to write out everything in longhand. Then in 1982 I got a computer. I can't imagine being without one now." She writes when she can these days, but she is always close to the house, waiting for a telephone call from the hospital to tell her that a lung for her husband Widdy's needed transplant has arrived. There's much to be done in the house and dogs to be taken care of, a pair of exceedingly frisky Dalmatians, one of whom is the recipient of Settle's unsettling whoop, "Get out of here, you bitch." Settle has a temper—and a rich sense of humor. In a copy of her longtime friend George Garrett's book *Understanding Mary Lee Settle*, she penned the inscription, "Whose husband requested the first copy." She has traveled widely, lived in Canada and Europe and around the United States, and she served three years in the Women's Auxiliary Air Force during World War II. She has written with passion and idealism through a career spanning five decades. Her first published novel, *The Love Eaters,* appeared in 1954. Her best-known works, the novels written over a twenty-six-year period comprising the Beulah Quintet, were drawn from memories and research and center on the use of history to portray the timeless struggle for personal and societal freedoms.

ANNE RIVERS SIDDONS grew up, she says, "with a life so typical Walt Disney might have done it." She was a homecoming queen and cheerleader in Fairburn, Georgia, a small town a few miles south of Atlanta where she was born and where her family has lived for six generations. She went to Auburn University where, in the dawning of the civil rights movement in the 1950s, she glimpsed a side to life beyond the parameters of her family traditions. Later, as editor of the then-new city magazine *Atlanta,* she decided to give writing a try. The result was her first book, a collection of essays, *John Chancellor Makes Me Cry,* in 1974 and two years later her first novel, *Heartbreak Hotel,* a coming-of-age story set in a small Southern university in the increasingly turbulent 1950s. With eleven novels to her credit now, she has become among the most popular and prolific of the chroniclers of the contemporary South, though she has used locales as varied as Maine and Italy for some of the stories. She greeted the photographer at the Buckhead home off Atlanta's Peachtree Road where she lives with her husband Heyward. The large and beautifully appointed home has a separate guest house where Siddons writes, and it was there she agreed to pose. From her desk in the high-ceilinged room, she can see a pair of photographs she says offer inspiration to her. One is an unpublished photograph of F. Scott Fitzgerald, the other a portrait of Bobby Kennedy made by Alfred Eisenstadt. One of her closest longtime friends is author Pat Conroy, who lived in Atlanta for a time and now visits her when he returns to the city. "Pat is a wonderful and incredibly generous person who gave me so many good ideas and encouragement when I was getting started writing." Siddons's most recent novels include *Fault Lines* (1995), *Downtown* (1994), and *Hill Towns* (1993).

DAVE SMITH sits on the back of the sofa in his living room and talks quietly and eloquently about his art: poetry. He suggested the living room for the photo rather than his usual writing space because one of his children has appropriated the room to prepare for an upcoming exam. Surrounded by books, many of them volumes of poetry, the athletic-looking Smith appears at ease with his life and the muse. Hailed as one of America's finest poets, the fifty-four-year-old native of Portsmouth, Virginia, now makes his home in Baton Rouge, Louisiana. There he is professor of English at LSU and serves as co-editor of the journal *Southern Review.* His literary output is staggering: twenty-three books since his first collection of poems, *Bull Island,* was released in 1970. There have been fifteen volumes of poetry since then, most recently *Fate's Kite,* which appeared in 1995. He also has acquired an enviable reputation for his teaching skills and his literary work as critic, editor, and essayist, and he has written a novel *Onliness* (1981). He was graduated from the University of Virginia and went to the University of Southern Illinois, where he wrote his master's thesis on the poetry of James Dickey. He first began to publish poems while serving in the Air Force and continued to produce volumes of poetry while acquiring his Ph.D. at Ohio University. He taught at a number of colleges and universities before coming to LSU in 1990. *Fate's Kite,* which brings together poems written between 1991 and 1995, is a tightly unified, brilliantly imaged collection of thirteen-line poems in which lost faith is played out against a backdrop of violent ecstasy and fierce disillusionment.

JULIE SMITH won an Edgar in 1991 for writing the best mystery novel, *New Orleans Mourning.* The Edgar—a statue of Edgar Allan Poe smaller in size than its prestige might suggest—now rests above her writing space on a shelf of honor flanked by framed photos of Tennessee Williams and William Faulkner. "That Edgar changed my life," says the lively red-haired author of a dozen novels. "It was the most exciting thing that has ever happened to me, except for my marriage, of course. Before that I was publishing regularly, but I was bankrupt. Now I could make a living after that." Born in Annapolis, Maryland, in 1944, Smith grew up in Savannah, Georgia, was graduated from Ole Miss and has lived in San Francisco and New Orleans most of the time since college. Living now with her husband Lee in a three-story home in New Orleans's famed French Quarter, she finds herself comfortably placed. "New Orleans is a wonderful place for writers. There's no conformity expected . . . I'm basically an outlaw at heart. If there's a rule, I want to break it." She does that with her writing, refusing to set a routine for getting her novels down on paper. "I write at night. I never start until 4 P.M. If I were to work all day, I'd get the same amount done as if I had worked just between 9 and 11 at night. That's when I'm the most creative." Her first published book, *Death Turns a Trick* (1983), featured attorney and amateur sleuth Rebecca Schwartz and a San Francisco setting. Schwartz showed up in two additional novels before Smith brought forth homicide detective Skip Langdon in her Edgar Award–winning book. Langdon has made several repeat appearances, most recently in *The Kindness of Strangers* (1996), which, like its predecessors, is set amid the "seductive perversity" of New Orleans. Smith was a journalist for much of her early career, writing for daily papers in New Orleans and San Francisco where she was among the first women on the staff. She also wrote three novels with a colleague that have never been published. "And with good reason," she says laughingly.

LEE SMITH, with her refreshing acceptance of self and others, has managed to avoid successfully the petty jealousies that can mar relationships—especially between writers. No one speaks ill of her, a remarkable feat given her longevity as a writer. In the home that she and her husband, the writer Hal Crowther, recently purchased in Hillsborough near Chapel Hill, North Carolina, she hosts a party for her friend the author Jill McCorkle to celebrate McCorkle's new novel. A group of writers from the vicinity show up to join in the festivities and heap praise on the new home. "We're really thrilled with it," Smith says, and the next morning, a beautifully sunny fall day, she eagerly guides the photographer around the yard to find the perfect location for his work. The smile seems to come as easily as the books. Her first novel, *The Last Day the Dogbushes Bloomed,* was published in 1968, and the most recent, her twelfth, *The Christmas Letters,* came out in 1996. They focus on the common folk of Appalachia, and all share a common element of birth. For each one, Smith has written the last sentence of the book first. "I guess that sounds crazy, but that's the way I've always done it. It gives me the long view, I suppose." Smith, fifty-two and a native of Grundy, Virginia, now writes in a second-story office (which was still unfinished when the photographer visited), giving her a view into the graceful, tree-shaded yard with a small pool and a gated garden that some joke is where some Heel writers are buried. "I have to practically have a gun to my head to force me to write. I hate it. It's work, so much work," she says emphatically. "If I had to sit down and write a certain number of pages a day, I'd write nothing but drivel. I write when I've got something to say."

ELIZABETH SPENCER has made her home in Chapel Hill, North Carolina, since 1986, after living for some time in Canada and Italy. "I really enjoy being back in the South," says the seventy-five-year-old writer, who was born and raised in Carrollton, Mississippi, where her ancestors have lived for well over a century. And the influence of the region has always been an important element in her creative output. She started writing in high school and won awards for her stories written while she was a student at Bellhaven College in Jackson. She was briefly a newspaper reporter before turning to writing full-time, and her first novel, *Fire in the Morning,* appeared in 1948. Since then she has produced a dozen novels and short-story collections, most recently *The Night Travellers* (1991). She not only greeted the photographer when he arrived at her home in September but demonstrated as well her legendary hospitality by fixing him dinner. She was photographed in her second-floor office, surrounded by some of the thousands of books that line shelves in several rooms in the house. "I didn't come early or easily to the computer," she says of her writing habits. "But I use it now. And I keep the typewriter for typing envelopes." Her manuscripts go to the National Library of Canada (she lived in Montreal for twenty-five years, beginning in 1958) because, "They approached me in the early 1980s, and our apartment was filling up with papers. I suppose it seems a little strange since I'm not really a Canadian writer, but I was flattered they were so interested." Probably her best-known book is the novella *The Light in the Piazza* (1960), which was later made into a film. Her *Collected Stories* was published in 1981 and brought her praise as one of the American masters of the short-story form, an author who writes with subtlety and sensitivity about the quest for individual freedom and the responsibility liberation entails.

MICKEY SPILLANE knows people are surprised to learn he has lived in South Carolina for forty-one years. The creator of the Mike Hammer hard-boiled detective series, honored as a Grand Master by the nation's mystery writers, a professional writer for more than a half century, one of the most familiar faces in American popular culture through his movie roles and beer commercials, Spillane at seventy-nine is still tough, still bursting with amusing stories, and still writing. Born in Brooklyn, he had the tough-guy face to go with the detective he brought to life in novels beginning with *I, the Jury* (1947); his hero has gone on to movies, television, and, most recently, comic books. Spillane lives with his wife in the quiet coastal fishing hamlet of Murrells Inlet in a house rebuilt after it was destroyed by Hurricane Hugo in 1989. Spillane enjoys an unobstructed view of the inlet waters from the wind-brushed veranda that runs across the second floor of the house. Spillane discovered the location when he flew over the Myrtle Beach area in his P-51 Mustang during World War II. He brought his family back for vacations, then bought a house in 1954 for fifteen thousand dollars at a time when he was already a best-selling legend. He does his writing now as he always has, on a Smith-Corona typewriter, in an office a few steps from the veranda, a small room filled with memorabilia, files, and photographs and a heater for writing in the chill of winter. Outside, by the waterway, is a covered enclave where he does television commercials and interviews, and underneath the house is "My toy," a 1956 Jaguar XK-140, a gift from John Wayne in gratitude for a Spillane movie script that year. Spillane doesn't worry about either he or Mike Hammer getting old: "There's nothing wrong with getting older. You just can't do everything you want. But believe me, there's plenty left."

JOHN STONE is a poet and physician of distinction, a combination that while not unique is nonetheless rare. He is professor of cardiology and associate dean and director of admissions at the Emory University School of Medicine in Atlanta. And he also gives lectures in the English department there. He posed for the photographer in his office at Emory, "A great place for me although it's a little cluttered," Stone, sixty, says. Some of the books on the shelves are about medical subjects, others deal with literature past and present. Stone has published three volumes of poetry, beginning with *The Smell of Matches* in 1972, which was followed by *In All the Rain* (1980) and *Renaming the Streets* (1985). He also wrote a book of essays in 1990, *In the Country of Hearts*, and co-edited *Principles and Practice of Emergency Medicine* in 1978. "It's easier to find the time to write poetry than prose. Poetry can be written in brief snatches of time. I carry 3 x 5 cards with me, and when the muse is talking, I can stop and quickly jot down what I need to," he says. Stone was born in Jackson, Mississippi, and grew up in the Texas town of Palestine ("pronounced just as you'd think"). Back in Jackson for high school, he was editor of the literary magazine, and one afternoon he hand-carried the entries in its literary competition to the home of a local woman who had agreed to judge them. "I handed them to this older woman who was very pleasant to me. It was about ten years later before I realized that woman was Eudora Welty," Stone recalls with a laugh. One of his happiest collaborations was co-editing an anthology of writings on literature and medicine, *On Doctoring,* now in its second edition, which is presented annually to every student entering a medical school in the United States.

WILLIAM STYRON won the Pulitzer Prize for Fiction for his 1967 novel *The Confessions of Nat Turner* and since 1951 has produced four other novels in addition to story collections, memoirs, and volumes of essays. It is a carefully considered output which has placed him among the finest of America's twentieth-century authors. At first reluctant to meet with the photographer because of previous bad experiences posing for others, Styron, seventy-one, soon is willingly discussing the creative process. Saying his writing space is "a mess, let's stay away from it," Styron chooses to sit for his picture in the living room of his large yellow country home in the rolling hills of southern Connecticut. With a postcard view of a pasture through the window, he explains that he works at "a deliberate pace," preferring to rise late and do his writing in longhand during the afternoon hours. Styron interrupts the session several times to walk into the kitchen where he is cooking chicken for dinner. The home—there are others in New York City and Martha's Vineyard—is filled with family memorabilia and photographs, many of them showing former President John F. Kennedy and Kennedy family members with Styron. Born in Newport News, Virginia, Styron served with the Marines in the Pacific during World War II, later studied writing at Duke University, and produced his first novel, *Lie Down in Darkness* (1951), winner of the prestigious Prix de Rome, while still a member of the Marine Reserves. Among his other books are *Sophie's Choice* (1979) and *Darkness Visible: A Memoir of Madness* (1990) in which Styron candidly and eloquently discusses his long struggle to overcome a deep depression that at one point left him on the verge of suicide.

MARGARET WALKER enjoys the rare distinction of living on a street named after her in Jackson, Mississippi. "I live in an historic area here," she says with a large grin. "This house is right between Martin Luther King Boulevard and Medgar Evers Street. Doesn't get any better." It has been over thirty years since her classic novel, *Jubilee,* appeared, a work which was decades in the creation. "I first heard the story from my grandmother when I was nineteen. I was a senior at Northwestern and decided I knew enough to write the story." It took her thirty years: "I was telling the story, not showing it." The book finally appeared in 1965 on her fiftieth birthday and satisfied her doctoral dissertation requirement from the University of Iowa. That novel, drawn from folklore and oral histories, offers vivid, complex portrayals of women in the context of historical slave life and has been called a realistic response to the romanticism of *Gone with the Wind.* It is just one of a number of books for Walker, who at eighty-one ("I don't look it, do I?") continues writing and research on an autobiography and volumes of essays and poetry. In the office in her home she proudly points the photographer to shelves of honors but makes it clear this is also a working space. Born in Birmingham, Alabama, in 1915, daughter of a minister of the African Methodist Episcopal Church, Walker notes that her energized pace has been tempered only because of the lingering effects of a stroke several years ago. "I have to write in longhand now. Because of the stroke I can't use either a typewriter or a word processor. So things go a little more slowly for me, but I'm not ready to quit. I've got nine grandchildren, too. Do I look like I'm ready to stop anything?"

EUDORA WELTY is eighty-seven, and there have been hints that the frailties of age have severely slowed her. She greets the photographer with bright eyes and curious mind, and it is quickly evident that this Mississippi-born author, honored as one of the great American writers of the twentieth century, retains her passion, her wit, and her generosity of spirit. "I feel pretty good these days," she answers her questioners. She uses the arm of a companion from nearby Millsaps College to help get around her house, the one in Jackson where she has lived almost continuously since 1931. "I don't have a car any more, of course. I used to love to get in it and drive. We went up to Yazoo City a lot. That was always fun." She isn't writing now—her arthritis is sometimes painful, preventing her from holding a pen—but writing is never far away. "I have some projects in my head." She pauses, then adds with a smile, "If worse came to worse, I'd write with my teeth." She talks about the photographs she made of African Americans in Mississippi in the 1930s, so revealing in their simplicity and intimacy: "I've always looked for the visual. That's how I write. A good writer has good eyes and good ears. Now my hearing is bad, and that's a curse." She owns more honors than most writers have books and confesses she has always loved the act of creating. "It's just talking about writing that's so hard for me." Before it's time to go, Miss Welty asks her guests if they'd like a drink. "You want some bourbon?" She accompanies the photographer to the door, which boasts a "Re-elect Clinton-Gore" sticker, and poses there with no evidence of diminished energy. "Let's dump Dole," she says with a smile.

144

MICHAEL LEE WEST was born in Louisiana but now resides in Lebanon, Tennessee, not far from Nashville. She and her husband had been living in a home they renovated from an old funeral parlor but moved into another "new old home" just a month before she agreed to meet the photographer at the 1996 Southern Festival of books in Nashville. "The house is a wreck. Boxes, stuff. I can't stand for anyone to see the mess now. Let's make the photograph somewhere else," she said. While posing on a warm autumn day, the forty-three-year-old author of three novels talked about her then-just-published book *American Pie,* a tangy story about three entangled sisters. "That title. People ask me about that. Well, of course I love food. I mean, look at me and why would you even ask that question?" She reminds listeners that her second novel, *She Flew the Coop* (1994), carried a food-related subtitle: *A Novel Concerning Life, Death, Sex, and Recipes in Limoges, Louisiana.* It contained a recipe for cantaloupe pickles, which young girls "In the old days called 'Can't Elope' pickles and avoided like the plague so we wouldn't be old maids." With a distinctive narrative voice and a literary imagination that resonates with vibrant, colorful, irreverent characters, she has become one of the rising stars of Southern writing. Her first book, the generation-spanning *Crazy Ladies,* was published to a chorus of praise in 1990. She admits to a fondness for reading magazines and in recent years has begun an interest in collecting first editions of modern fiction.

BAILEY WHITE was born in a Thomasville, Georgia, hospital, but that's about the only time she's been away from the home where she lives in "way south Georgia." To get to it the photographer needed specific directions to the house about a half mile off a deserted highway. There, amid a thousand acres, White lives, writes, and gardens. "At least I can do a little more gardening now while I'm writing instead of teaching," she says. She is taking a couple of years from her duties as an elementary school teacher to write her second book, a series of connected stories that "doesn't look like it's going to wind up as a novel," she says. Her first book, *Mama Makes Up Her Mind,* a collection of essays, magazine pieces, and radio broadcasts, was published in 1993: "But that hardly seemed like a book to me. It was just a bunch of things I'd done." White, forty-six, came to national attention in 1991 when she began regularly reading her commentaries on National Public Radio. Those funny, easy-going stories of the simple life she and her mother lived in rural Georgia attracted a large and enthusiastic following, and White found herself the recipient of hundreds of letters every month. "It's slowed to a trickle now since I'm writing and not doing the broadcasts as frequently," she says. She awakens early in the day—"My best time"—to begin her writing, completing the first draft on an old manual typewriter sitting on a table in the kitchen. "I try to get in a few good hours every day and try to get something completed at the end of each week, a chapter or so. But writing isn't fun for me. The fun starts after you're done." Preparing her scripts for broadcast takes much less effort: "Those go pretty quickly, and I'm usually done in a day or so." She chatted cheerfully while having her photograph made, wearing jeans and a monogrammed shirt—though the monogram isn't hers. "I bought the shirt at the Goodwill store," she explains.

148

JAMES WILCOX agreeably consented to pose outdoors on a cold, blustery, over-cast December afternoon in Madison Square Park, not far from his apartment on Manhattan's Lower East Side. Behind him is New York's historic Flatiron Building, a site Wilcox, forty-seven, suggested for the photographer "because it really looks so much like New York City." Though he is comfortable living in Manhattan—he's been there for nearly twenty-five years—he is never far from his roots in the South. He was born in Hammond, Louisiana, a town not unlike the fictional Tula Springs, the setting for four of his six novels. His father holds a doctor-ate in music, and Wilcox was a musician in high school, commuting to Baton Rouge to play cello with the city's symphony orchestra. "It was fun, but it also helped me develop a sense of structure which has been useful in my writing." He credits his mother with instilling in him a love of reading. He went to Yale University—"I was lonely, it was cold, and boy, was that an academic challenge for a little kid from Hammond"—where he took a writing seminar with Robert Penn Warren. And Warren, twice a Pulitzer Prize–winner, offered high praise on the dust jacket of Wilcox's first novel, *Modern Baptists* (1983). Wilcox was an editorial assistant and an editor at Random House and at Doubleday in New York before turning to writing. "I don't mind being called a Southern writer at all," he says, "But it's not something I go around talking about. I'm happy to be here because it gives me a better perspective on things Southern. And maybe when I'm back home I get a little better perspective on New York, too." His nov-els—most recently *Guest of a Sinner* in 1993—are infused with a comic spirit and a distinctly Southern flavor and perhaps resemble modern-day novels of manners in their tone.

MILLER WILLIAMS was busy preparing the poem he would read at President Bill Clinton's second inaugural ceremonies when he agreed to meet the photographer in late December. He posed in his office at the University of Arkansas Press in Fayetteville, where he has been director since 1980. "There's not much free time right now," he says behind a desk full of manuscripts and paperwork waiting for his attention. That means he works on his poem at night, usually beginning around 10 P.M. and continuing sometimes until 2 A.M. Williams, sixty-six, has always preferred to write his first words with a fountain pen on a legal pad, sitting in a large, overstuffed chair at home. He does his editing, however, on a computer. A multitalented man of letters, a poet and translator, Williams was born in Hoxie, Arkansas, earned degrees in biology and zoology, and taught science in college for twelve years. With encouragement from John Ciardi, he began writing poetry and published his first collection, *A Circle of Stone,* in 1964. Since then, he has produced nine books of poetry to go with fifteen volumes of criticism, translation, and anthology, one of them a study of his mentor, Ciardi. As press director, he has initiated a publishing program that includes fiction as well as nonfiction, and he has the distinction of publishing the first book of fiction by Ellen Gilchrist, *In the Land of Dreamy Dreams,* in 1981. Though he has no academic degrees in English or formal training in literature, he has taught English and foreign languages at colleges in the United States, Chile, and Mexico and founded the *New Orleans Review* at Loyola University. One of his three children is Lucinda Williams, the country singer.

CHRISTINE WILTZ wrote three novels before most readers knew she was a female author. "The publisher deliberately passed me off as a man. They used 'Chris Wiltz' on the jacket. There was no photograph of me and no personal pronoun. And my detective was a man," she says. "Even when they did put a photo of me on the book, some people never got the message. I got tired of being addressed as a man." Readers couldn't miss her gender, however, when Wiltz came out with her fourth book, the much-praised novel *Glass House* (1994), published by her home-state press in Baton Rouge. "I had given the book to LSU and forgotten about it, and one day they sent me a letter and said they'd like to publish it." When they did, her photograph and the name Christine Wiltz on the jacket left no doubts. She was born in New Orleans and has lived all but two of her years there, finishing her formal education in California. She held a variety of jobs after college: at the drug rehab center at Tulane University, as a bookseller in New Orleans, and as a short-order cook. Wiltz, forty-nine, also picked up a black belt in karate along the way. "Somewhere in there I knew I wanted to write. It hadn't occurred to me I could do it for a living. Then I read Raymond Chandler, and that really turned me on." Her first book, *The Killing Circle* (1981), featured a Chandler-like private investigator in New Orleans, Neal Rafferty. "I remember getting my first royalty check, for a thousand dollars, and my agent told me, 'That won't make much of a living.' And I thought, 'Who says?' Of course, it turned out he was right," she says laughing. She was photographed in the writing space of her Uptown New Orleans home where "I try to write every day. The book gets done a lot faster that way." Heading into 1997, she was beginning work on her first nonfiction book, about the last madam in New Orleans, who ran brothels in the city for more than forty years before her death in 1974.

C. VANN WOODWARD is the preeminent twentieth-century historian of the American South. The author or editor of nearly two dozen books, he is the recipient of every major American history award: the Pulitzer, Bancroft, and Parkman prizes. He also has served as president of the American Historical Association, the Organization of American Historians, and the Southern Historical Association. Now eighty-two, the native of tiny Vanndale, Arkansas, lives near New Haven since his retirement from Yale University in 1977. At his home on a ridge where he lives alone, he welcomes the photographer into his office in the basement. There he continues to work on a 1930s-era manual typewriter in the dark, book-lined space that appears unusually well organized. A photograph of William Faulkner is on the wall, and nearby is a row of pipes, unsmoked: "They are an inspiration for resistance," the quiet, genteel Woodward says with a smile. He was teaching at the University of Florida when his first book was published in 1938, *Tom Watson: Agrarian Rebel*, a biography of the turn-of-the-century populist Georgia politician. Later teaching at Johns Hopkins, then Yale, Woodward produced books that won him acclaim and honors around the world: *Origins of the New South, 1877–1913* (1951), *The Strange Career of Jim Crow* (1955), and *The Burden of Southern History* (1960) among them. His editing of the well-known journals of South Carolinian Mary Chesnut in *Mary Chesnut's Civil War* received the Pulitzer Prize in 1982. Woodward has been both scholar and activist in behalf of the downtrodden in the South. His writings have influenced legions of young historians, and his interpretations of Southern history, particularly from the post–Civil War years to the mid-twentieth century, have become accepted in texts and classes throughout the nation.